HIRE *with*
FIRE

THE RELATIONSHIP-DRIVEN INTERVIEW AND HIRING METHOD

Denise Wilkerson, BSN, MHRD, SPHR
Randy Wilkerson, MBA, CPC

This is a work of nonfiction.

No part of this book may be reproduced or transmitted or transferred in any form or by any means, graphic, electronic, mechanical, including photocopying, recording, taping or by any information storage retrieval system or device, without the permission in writing by the author.

This book provides information from many sources, including personal experiences. It does not contain all information available on the subject. Information herein is provided and sold with the knowledge the publisher and author does not offer legal advice. If legal advice is needed, consult with the appropriate professional. Every effort has been made to make this book as accurate as possible. However, there may be typographical or content errors. Therefore, this book should serve only as a general guide and not as the ultimate source of subject information. This book has not been created to be specific to any individual's or organizations' situation or needs. This book contains information to educate and entertain. The author and publisher shall have no liability or responsibility to any person or entity regarding any loss or damage incurred, or alleged to have incurred, directly or indirectly, by the information contained in this book.

Links to websites are provided for informational purposes only and do not constitute endorsement of products or services. Links are subject to change, expiration, or redirection without notice. Author or publisher receives no commission from linked websites upon accessing websites or upon purchase of products or services.

Cover Design – Jaycee DeLorenzo
Cover Photos – DepositPhotos
Publishing Coordinator – Sharon Kizziah-Holmes

Dandyworx
Productions

Published by Dandyworx Productions

This book is available at quantity discounts for bulk purchases.
For information, call 1-877-370-2462

ISBN -13: 978-1-7332611-0-4

DEDICATION

This book is dedicated to all the relationship-driven hiring managers we have worked with over the past two decades who have shown empathy towards the candidates they interviewed. Through your kindness you change lives by empowering people. Your time spent coaching, listening, respecting and valuing the individual did not go unnoticed. You make a difference every day in the lives of others, whether you hire them or not.

HIRE with FIRE is also dedicated to our mothers, Anneliese Cottiers and Romalee Wilkerson - two energetic, empowering, and entertaining strong women who encouraged us in every endeavor.

ACKNOWLEDGMENTS

First, we want to thank God for giving us the strength, knowledge, temperament and ability to complete this work. We are blessed in our relationship with Him.

Thank you to each one of the following individuals for their help with Hire with Fire. We couldn't have done it without you!

Sharon Kizziah-Holmes-Publishing Coordinator

Holly Atkinson and Peter Archer- Editing & Review

Carlos Lemos-Illustrations

Jaycee DeLorenzo-Cover and Book Design

Sherry Haney-Website and Technical Support

In addition, we appreciate the participation and contribution of our panel of hiring managers. We were fortunate to have this group of professionals to help us by sharing their insight.

A special thank you to Martin Yate, Author of *Hiring the Best* and the *Knock 'em Dead* book series for his words of encouragement and support.

Many others have encouraged us in the writing of Hire with Fire! Thanks to our friends, family, and business associates who have helped along the way with content, direction and sometimes, humor!

We hope you enjoy Hire with Fire!

CONTRIBUTORS:
PANEL OF HIRING MANAGERS

Throughout this book, you will read quotes from fifteen leading management professionals in areas such as healthcare, education, information technology, city government, hospitality, and banking and financial services.

With experience in human resources, sales, and management, each of these individuals has interviewed, hired, and led teams. We selected these individuals because of their leadership experience and expertise. We have personally worked with each of these individuals and feel their leadership style represents the concepts of HIRE with FIRE.

We would like to thank each of them for taking time to contribute their thoughts and ideas.

Matt Aultman, *District Manager, six years' hiring experience, Pharmaceutical Sales*

Tracy Barry, *Sr. HR Partner, fifteen-plus years' hiring experience, Medical Device, Pharmaceuticals, Financial Services, and Publishing*

Greg Burris, *President & CEO, United Way of the Ozarks, thirty years' hiring experience, Non-profit, Higher Education, City Government- former City Manager for the City of Springfield, Missouri*

Mike DeMuth, *Vice President Sales, fifteen years' hiring experience, Healthcare Information Technology*

Mike Denker, *Area Sales Director, twenty-four years' hiring experience, Medical Device and Software*

Todd Derickson, *Director of Sales, twenty-plus years' hiring experience, Medical Device*

Brent Dunn, *Vice-President, Office of University Advancement, Executive Director of Missouri State University Foundation, thirty-five years' hiring experience, Higher Education*

David Eberson, *Vice President Commercialization, Sales and Service, North America, twenty-five years' hiring experience, Medical Device and Pharmaceuticals*

Steve Ford, *Senior Manager of New Market Development, twenty-plus years' hiring experience, Pharmaceuticals, Capital Equipment, and Medical Device*

Tom Fowler III, *Senior Vice President, State Bank of Southwest Missouri, twenty-three years' hiring experience, Banking*

Seda Onek, *Human Resources Manager, ten-plus years' experience, Medical Device*

Reggie Steward, *Regional Sales Director, two years' hiring experience, Medical Sales*

Rita Wright Gurian, *Retired Healthcare Executive – Current Non-Profit & Professional Development Coach, thirty-plus years' hiring experience, Healthcare and Non-Profit*

Marc Waldman, *Vice President Business Development, twenty years' hiring experience, Medical Device*

Ericca Zumaya, *Human Excellence Generalist, two years' hiring experience in Life Sciences/Biotechnology*

CONTENTS

PREFACE

HIRE with FIRE is about building great relationships with the people you interview. We believe the employee-employer relationship actually starts the moment the candidate is contacted about a position, whether that is by email, phone or a face-to-face interaction. The initial contact made by your company, through human resources or a hiring manager, sets the tone and stirs the candidate's interest in a potential job opportunity.

Throughout the interview process, the employer and potential employee will meet to get to know each other better. During this time, they may experience a variety of different feelings similar to the emotions involved in a dating relationship—the nervous energy of meeting someone for the first time, the awkwardness of getting to know each other, or the worry about their first impression. Interviewing, just like dating, involves feelings. By definition, feelings are an emotional state or reaction. Sometimes those feelings bring insecurity. Oftentimes, if we are lucky, they bring us reassurance, enthusiasm, and passion. Either way, as human beings, our feelings are an important part of who we are. Although we hate to admit it, our feelings can change our destiny and can cause us to move forward or turn back. Our emotions often guide us into knowing whether or not an anticipated change, such as a career move or a candidate hire, is going to benefit us or cause us peril. This instinctual feeling is known as our gut reaction.

In *HIRE with FIRE*, we will look at how gut reaction can influence our decisions, and we will discuss how your emotions may influence your decision on who you hire. We will also take a closer look into the candidate's feelings during the interview process and the impact it has on their decision to accept a job offer, their onboarding experience, and their longevity with your company. We believe the relationship-driven interview and hiring method is a personal, respectful, and empowering approach to how you behave or deal with candidates throughout the interview and hiring process. The relationship side of candidate selection, the job offer, and final acceptance by the candidate are all equally important and necessary components of hiring quality employees.

In *HIRE with FIRE*, we approach these elements in a personal and respectful manner by attempting to build the employment relationship instead of just *making a hire*. Although mindful of the legalities and complexities of modern hiring, we believe it can still be a fun and rewarding experience.

Randy and I have been recruiters for over two decades. We own an executive search firm where we recruit various professionals. We enjoy working with our clients and assisting candidates in finding career opportunities. As a result of our experiences, we have gained insight into the employer-employee relationship.

As we discuss some of our personal and professional stories and relate them to the hiring process, we hope that you will find a few minutes to sit back, relax, and enjoy the fire.

All the best,

Denise and Randy

CHAPTER ONE

Setting the Scene

It can be exhausting to find the right match! Just trying to find the sock that matches the one you took out of the dryer can drive you crazy. Finding a good match for anything can be difficult, let alone trying to find your soulmate or even trying to find the best talent for your company.

As recruiters, we are looking for talent. It's what we do, and we love it. We are tasked to find the right people for our clients every day. Similar to a dating app that matches compatible individuals, a recruiting company screens candidates to see if they are the right match for a company's open position. This isn't always easy because every person and job is unique. Additionally, every candidate has a different background and a different story to tell. So we started thinking…which led to this book. And maybe you are thinking about it too since you've picked it up! So here we are, ready to embark on our new relationship.

Relationship? But wait, we may have never met! Yes, I know this sounds odd, but we are going to spend some time together over the next few chapters, and you don't spend time with just anyone. Typically, if you spend time with someone, it's because it benefits you in some way.

We can probably agree that relationships are important and exist at every level, even globally. Think about it this way: if two countries can be in a relationship, why can't we? During wartime, relationships were critical to our country's success. It's great to have allies.

The word *relationship* may mean something different to each of us. Dictionaries often describe it as "a state of affairs existing between those having relations or dealings."[1] It is an association, connection, a liaison, or affinity for someone or something. Friendship is a great example.

We have found over the last two decades of working in the recruiting business that new employees have a higher success rate when a relationship is created early between the interviewer and the candidate. This relationship often continues throughout the interview process into employment. It is the basis for *HIRE with FIRE: The Relationship-Driven Interview and Hiring Method.*

---

[1]Merriam-Webster, https://www.merriam-webster.com/dictionary/relationship, Accessed August 23, 2019

Through years of our recruitment experience, we have observed a strong similarity between a personal courting relationship and the relationship that develops during the hiring process. As we discuss relationships further, we want you to consider looking at the hiring process from a different perspective—as if it were a dating relationship. For example, the first interview has some similarities to that all-important first date. Both parties may be nervous, anxious, and anticipating the next moment. They may *click* with the other person or they may not. This is not unlike those important first few minutes of an interview. Is a personal relationship any different? The key elements of human interaction are present in both scenarios. But since we want you to read on, we will save that information for later.

It is our hope that through the *HIRE with FIRE* method, you will gain a better understanding of the feelings and interpersonal interactions that help both the interviewer and the candidate have a better understanding of one another. By exposing the potential areas of opportunity or concern, we hope you will develop a stronger relationship with each person you interview, not just those you hire.

In addition, since this book is about relationships, we will focus our discussions about the relationship that develops with each candidate you interview. Although extremely important to our discussions, for the purposes of this book, we will not extensively discuss diversity initiatives. However, we believe that for good relationships to exist within your organization and its culture, your company should have a well-defined diversity and inclusion plan. We must acknowledge that above everything else, all human beings are created equal, and good relationships, built on inclusivity can occur naturally when respect is offered to people of every race, color, religion, sex (including pregnancy, gender identity, and sexual orientation), national origin, age, disability or genetic information.

In our discussions, we are going to make the assumption that you already understand the important guidelines set by The U.S. Equal Employment Opportunity Commission (EEOC) and the Uniform

Guidelines on Employee Selection Procedures. If you have not been trained in these guidelines, go to the EEOC's website to familiarize yourself with them. Specifically, we want to point out, the importance of their guidelines on adverse impact, and the $4/5^{ths}$ or 80 percent rule during the selection process. However unintentional, your decisions, hiring practices, and policies should never disproportionately impact a protected group in a negative way. And though we have and will continue to use the dating metaphor, we are not trying to make light of dating relationships or the hiring process. Nor are we, in any way, trying to insinuate that you should date the people you interview. We all know that there are many issues that take place in the workplace related to sexual harassment and other types of discriminatory behavior that may occur. These are serious issues that should always be cause for concern and not taken lightly.

As a hiring manager, relative to how you treat prospects, you have two choices. You can either empower the candidates you interview or dismiss them, potentially making them feel devalued. It is our contention that every person should be treated with respect and dignity. Each person you meet has a unique story. Some candidates are happy with their current job but want to move up in their career. Maybe their current job offers no vertical advancement. Others may be unemployed, underemployed, downsized, or even have been terminated for cause. Each person will bring their own set of challenges to the interview. While you are not their career coach, you are a leader in your industry and what you say and do may have a strong impact. Throughout *HIRE with FIRE*, we hope that you will see interviewing as more than a task—it is an opportunity to make a difference in the lives of others.

In the course of our work, we also discovered that many of the successful candidates we have placed had several traits in common. This book is based on those discoveries. It's a method we call *HIRE with FIRE*.

To learn more about *HIRE with FIRE*, we will discuss hiring from an organizational perspective and then move to the candidate perspective. This process will help us move from a macro to a micro view relative to your current overall organizational needs and the needs of your team. Once the basic needs and organizational components are established, it becomes much more apparent on how to align departments, positions, and subsequent job descriptions relative to developing your company's staff. This, in effect, provides a detailed roadmap to move your organization and your team successfully into the future!

As a hiring manager, there are two ways to implement the *HIRE with FIRE* method into your organization's hiring processes. The first is on the organizational level, and the second is on a candidate level.

On an organizational level, *HIRE with FIRE* can help you and your leadership team organize your thoughts during periods of rapid growth within your company. The *HIRE with FIRE* method starts with a chapter on hiring plans which will assist you in assessing the needs of your organization. Following that is a chapter on identifying the key skills (pillars) necessary within a position prior to launching a candidate search. This book concludes with several chapters about interviewing and building strong relationships with employees to create a company culture that is filled with enthusiasm and passion.

On the candidate level, the *HIRE with FIRE* interview and selection method will challenge you to think differently about the people you interview and your relationship with them. As previously discussed, we believe relationships are formed during this critical stage, starting with the first interview.

In the course of reading this book, you will notice that we spell out the word *FIRE* and use this acronym to help you remember certain traits that we feel are important during the interview process. These letters are the basis for the *HIRE with FIRE* method. In the following chapters, you will learn more about what each letter represents and why it is important to both interviewing and hiring.

The acronym FIRE offers four key traits: functionality, integrity, results, and enthusiasm. We believe the most successful and productive employees have these traits, and analyzing the traits helps you quickly select outstanding talent from hundreds of resumes. Without these traits, certain tasks may not get done—or worse yet—may be completed incorrectly. Keep in mind we chose the word *FIRE* because it can also mean that someone is passionate or "on fire" about something, and we all want employees who are passionate and engaged about their work.

CHAPTER TWO

The Road to a Great Hire

The road to success is lined with obstacles. One obstacle a growing company may face is the challenge of hiring the right people for the right positions at the right time. Because of this, it is important to develop a hiring plan for your company.

A hiring plan is like a road map—it keeps you on track so you can arrive quickly at your destination. Maybe you think you know where you are going so you don't feel you need a map to get there. Some people are just really good with directions; others (like me) are directionally challenged. My husband, Randy, is good with directions most of the time. He likes to tell me when we travel that he "knows this area like the back of his hand." Although he says this to me only when he really doesn't have a clue about where we are but just wants me to relax.

Hiring is very similar to traveling. You must have a destination, a plan, and a course to follow in finding and selecting quality candidates. Think about your last vacation. Without directions and a plan, your travels could have been much different. Lack of planning makes traveling expensive and wastes time. When we talk about major events like extended travel, it becomes clear that without some sort of itinerary, there will be wrong turns, numerous stops, major delays, and other unnecessary hurdles that can have a real negative impact on the trip. The same lack of appropriate planning may deliver the same poor results when it comes to your hiring decisions.

The Hiring Plan

Without a solid forecast of organizational needs, it's virtually impossible for a company to grow in an efficient manner or at all. Every day, we talk to companies that have a significant market share within their industry. The potential for an increased market share is theirs to capture, but they can't figure out how to get it done. A quality hiring plan can address key concerns of hiring the right personnel with the ability and experience to get the job done. In this chapter, we will discuss the importance of developing a hiring plan for your organization.

As recruiters, we work with many companies. Over the years, we have had companies contact us to recruit candidates for open positions, only to decide midway through recruitment that they need to select internally or that the position wasn't needed at all. In one case, we had candidates scheduled to fly into the company's corporate office for the final interview only to have the company cancel. We later heard that they had decided to do a company-wide reorganization. The candidates were deflated and lost interest in ever working for that company again.

There may be situations in which this sort of thing is unavoidable, but there can be ramifications when companies decide to put a position on hold. Again, in this situation, candidates lose interest in ever working for the company and are left to wonder about the organization's stability.

If this was a dating scenario, it would be described as "commitment issues." If you are uncertain whether you will be filling the position, then don't ask a candidate to interview. No one wants to invest time in something that won't pan out. It's like dating someone who doesn't want to be in a relationship. We have found that most candidates want employment right now, not months later. Because of this, we can't stress enough the importance of knowing why you are hiring and making sure you are committed to the hiring plan.

How do you develop a hiring plan? Dividing these HR decisions into organizational (company) and individual (candidate) components may help. Simply put, we can determine these components to be the *who*, *what*, *when*, *where*, and *why*. Let's call these the 5 Ws.

The 5 W's, often attributed to the philosopher Aristotle, can help us organize our thoughts and plans relative to hiring plans. Just like your favorite detective, you will systematically arrive at thoughtful decisions by following an orchestrated plan.

How to Plan: The 5 W's of Hiring

Who

Let's first look at *who* should interview and hire. If you're not an HR professional, this is the time to bring this resource to the table. Allowing your HR professionals to be a part of these decisions is critical. They are educated and trained to have a global view of the entire hiring process and can help identify all aspects, from reviewing qualified candidates to identifying the candidate's potential impact upon the organization.

Organizational leaders normally look departmentally for thought leaders—those who are experienced and recognized in their discipline. The human resources area represents the professionals adept at managing organizational change and development. The HR group can be a huge ally throughout this process. Many organizations have found that bringing their HR partners in late, or not at all, is a detriment when hiring individuals. It is just good business practice to be more inclusive.

Relative to other thought leaders within your organization—if your project deals with the sales department, then look within your company for those with experience in past successful sales roles. They can help you assess what *good* looks like—or, better yet, what *great* looks like! Involve those in business operations and use their analytics in sales forecasting, expense management, future data analysis, and the market competition.

Although highly competent in what it does, the HR department is sometimes expected to be everything to everyone. Years ago, the HR group was thought of as simply "Payroll." Their perceived role was that of primarily dispersing salary and wages. Now, in a more executive role, HR oversees many different functions, programs and benefits. These areas include healthcare, vacation, sick time and family leave, arbitration between employees and management, new employee recruitment, developing job descriptions, along with publishing various policies and procedures. Empower this group to help. Again, bring in the troops! My father-in-law used to say, "There is safety in numbers." Generally speaking, the more individuals that view and interact with a candidate, the better the assessment you will have. Identify any and all of those people who can help you determine the successful direction of positions, personalities, and the key drivers that will help turn your hiring project into a great success!

Determining the right candidate is critical in virtually all hiring decisions. With the proper inputs relative to a potential employee's attributes, education, and experiences, HR professionals can help guide you—not only with the criteria for the position as outlined in the roles and responsibilities, but also those individual traits and backgrounds that may fit the needs of your particular opening. Working together with HR, outside recruiters, or maybe internal referrals can help you land a great fit. By the way, finding a great fit and a good hire will make you look good—and will help your career.

What

Now, on to the *what*. The *what* in our scenario is simply the proposed role or position itself. This can be a new or existing role, but it needs to be defined in advance. To do this, most companies use a job description. A job description outlines *what* the job is and *what* is required of the employee. We will discuss this more in depth in the next chapter.

When

Now let's look closer at the *when* of our scenario. To do this, we need to discuss forecasting. To forecast is to make a prediction or best guess based upon an analysis of relevant facts. It can be difficult predicting the future of your human capital needs. Whether you are using quantitative data-driven methods or the more subjective qualitative processes, it's much like predicting the stock market or your local weather—the outcome is only as good as the input data, and that can change at a moment's notice. Therefore, you will need to analyze your human capital needs by forecasting the potential rewards and the risks. Yes, this sometimes is easier said than done.

For healthcare professionals, the ability to forecast your staffing needs is critical to each patient's care. When I managed nurses, predicting staffing needs was difficult as the patient census fluctuated. When the census was high (that is, when there were a lot of patients), I would request that nurses work extra shifts; when the census was low, I would ask them to take the day off. Most nurses are used to working flexible schedules, but most companies do not operate this way.

Forecasting human capital needs is a crucial HR function. Your company is hiring individuals who are key to the organization's success. We hear discussions about *key* individuals, but we have to assume that all employees are *key* individuals—at least that's the initial goal. Most businesses don't need non-essential personnel— they need individual contributors.

As we've discussed, some forecasts are very well thought out and calculated, using the latest, elaborate software programs. Others are handed down by a board or experienced C-level committee with years of experience. Both are good methodologies and represent sound judgments in many cases. Joining these two methodologies of forecasting can make your forecasts a commonsense procedure and provide the organization outstanding benefits. By using that idea, an HR department can develop a multifaceted approach that integrates the quantitative data-driven forecasting software and then incorporates the organization's experienced personnel. This combines a qualitative and quantitative approach by bringing in the years of humanistic judgment based upon C-level experience and then applying the quantitative forecasting methods. The goal is to achieve the best of both forecasting methods.

Again, you and your staff are detectives along the way, searching to find the right people for the right jobs at the right location and at the right time. Yes, the stars will align! You're looking into the future, staring down the road to determine HR needs. You have to consider a plethora of variables when making decisions. These decisions touch virtually every element of the organization. Some of the decisions within your organization will be stellar and some not so much. However, like forecasting the weather, nothing is a certainty in business.

Where

We are now ready to discuss *where* to hire. This is particularly important in sales. It involves positioning current and future personnel in the right geographic locations. Planning can be based upon proximity to the corporate office, demand relative to certain geographic area, access to manufacturing or a marketing unit, or a variety of other considerations. There can and will be many thoughts when you assess an individual candidate or hire an entire staff in a specific area. Placing your personnel in the right location to optimize their time and efforts can be crucial to a company's bottom line.

Relative to geography, taking the time to do a complete territory or market analysis is paramount to generating an appropriate forecast. By forecasting your needs, you are helping to create your overall strategic plan. Failing to forecast or providing an incomplete HR forecast can lead to hiring at the wrong time, the wrong location, or for the wrong role. In retrospect, a good question might be, "Will the market sustain this part of our organization and offer us some degree of growth and opportunity in the immediate future if we lose part of our forecasted business?"

Why

Before you begin talking about hiring for an open position with your company, let's start by asking a question that doesn't always get asked: why are you hiring? That seems like a simple question, doesn't it? Maybe someone left the position or your company is growing or you are short staffed. Positions often get filled without consideration of the organization's immediate or long-term needs.

Answering the question of why you are hiring seems simple. However, a careful review of the company's human capital needs should be done on a continual basis to avoid critical staffing situations. The last thing you want to do is hire an employee and then realize you didn't need someone in that position. Due to poor organizational planning, we all probably know someone who has been laid off or downsized. It creates a tough time for everyone involved. This is why creating a strategic plan for human capital is important for any growing organization.

Once again, you should seek input from those key stakeholders (management) of the department seeking the positions. Quizzing them of their needs and potential outcomes will help justify the need for the position and solidify the future steps in the potential hiring process.

As a manager or HR associate, you need to understand as much about your organization as possible, but sometimes the corporate culture stands in the way. The C-Level often pushes for the next steps in the marketing or promotional program but may lack complete analysis. Their experience, drive, passion, and past successes sometimes create a gut response to move ahead and complete a task regarding a marketing effort or project. Many times, this works beautifully. Sometimes it doesn't.

How often should you review your human capital needs? We asked our panel of hiring managers to give us their thoughts.

"These days, one could argue an organization needs to assess its human capital needs on a daily basis because things are changing so quickly. A quarterly assessment is probably more reasonable. The massive demographic change that is underway is creating a situation where this assessment is no longer optional."

Greg Burris, President & CEO, United Way of the Ozarks, thirty years' hiring experience, Non-profit, Higher Education, City Government- former City Manager for the City of Springfield, Missouri

"Every six months, plan to review what is needed and also during that time assess for skill sets that are needed for the future five and ten years out. Make a plan for how you will introduce those skills into the organization— whether you need to buy it or make it."
Tracy Barry, Sr. HR Partner, fifteen-plus years' hiring experience, Medical Device, Pharmaceuticals, Financial Services, and Publishing

"While it is important to do an annual business plan to identify business needs and strategize headcount requirements, I believe that this process has to also be a dynamic process. Business needs and the economic climate changes every day. It is important to leverage your employees in the right roles, focus on their strengths and strategize your headcount."

Seda Onek, Human Resources Manager, ten-plus years' experience, Medical Device

"If you have the opportunity to Manage by Walking Around, this is a continuous activity. If you rely on reporting, it should be a weekly question, 'What are the greatest opportunities and highest payoff projects we're working on? Do we have the right people to make the most of each?'"

Mike Denker, Area Sales Director, twenty-four years' hiring experience, Medical Device and Software

> **"This should be an ongoing evaluation as needed. A company usually does yearly evaluations but in today's world, it is now as needed and ongoing to promote faster performance and based on company needs."**
>
> *Todd Derickson, Director of Sales, twenty-plus years' hiring experience, Medical Device*

Launching Products: Research, Development and Pipelines

Some markets have become increasingly complicated and data might be old by the time it's published, especially in the technology sector. Consumers and businesses alike demand the latest technologies including speed, productivity, and a whole host of other features and benefits. The sheer speed of our society basically dictates the need for effective research and development. Those companies that effectively manage this part of their organization win.

What is research and development? It is the very early stages of an organization's plans for specific products and services that are being developed and potentially offered. It involves market research into what customers want and need. Research and Development (R&D) is highly important, but somewhat uncertain to the company. At this point, a company may not be absolutely sure that a concept or product will be viable. R&D is risky due to the expense of initial research and total lack of a guarantee of a positive outcome. Still, it is necessary to survey the market to assess opportunities that facilitate launching new products. In a forecasting model, it is difficult to project future opportunities without a strong research and development component.

A strong research and development effort needs to be in place to bring about products to enter the product pipeline, but the product pipeline possesses a more immediate opportunity for sales and marketing. This importance comes from the fact that the product entering the product pipeline is generally past the development phase and expected to soon be marketable.

Both research and development and a company's pipeline are important, but of the two, the pipeline generally reflects the most immediate product marketing opportunity, since the product is in an approvable state and is almost ready to market. The company usually envisions the income opportunity and has estimated the potential initial revenue bump.

Many times products can be delayed, or in the medical world, not approved. This can drastically change the company's revenue projections, the number of individuals hired, and the scope of other ancillary hiring activities. Still, if there are enough products in the pipeline with significant research and development activities backing future endeavors, organizations can realign and grow significantly.

In today's business models, human capital needs are usually based on *product pipelines* and *research and development*. Sometimes, legitimate questions come up in forecasting: Has this product or service been fully developed? Does the research and development support the entry into the product pipeline? Are we ready to launch?

These questions brings us back to the *why*. What are the conditions within the market, and how is the organization poised to address them? Maybe it is time to hire a management and sales staff to sell the new products brought forth from the research and development department! That would address the *why* in that someone, probably at the C-level in marketing or sales department, is forecasting the need based upon data analysis and experience.

We hear the terms *product pipeline* and *research and development* used often in a speculative fashion, generally discussing future offerings of products or services. We know it's critically important to know where a company is in its product life cycle and what the future may hold.

Products are not static; they age and become antiquated and obsolete. A prime example is the typewriter. A once-booming piece of business equipment has virtually vanished in use today. Companies that sold this type of equipment and other ancillary services to large corporations and government—supporting their *typing pools* and other business units—are now gone. More recently, we've seen this scenario with the telephone. Our culture is no longer tied to communication via a wire. Like the landline, a company that remains the same without new product introduction falls behind and eventually fails. It takes a tremendous effort just to keep up the pace, let alone become a market leader.

However you determine your hiring needs, it will be very difficult for your organization to grow without a solid forecast of organizational needs relative to your human capital. Yes, there are many variables to consider at every level, but plans need to be put in place and changes should occur only when they are legitimate and verified by appropriate data and personnel. There are no certainties even in the best forecasting. It might be best to err on the side of fiscal conservatism.

The 5 Ws help you create a good HR avenue to assess and forecast the need for your personnel. It is essential to involve HR and the other key stakeholders at each level, from the creation of the job description to the onboarding of your new employee. If you clearly and definitively follow through and have a solid forecast for personnel, then your efforts should produce a great hiring event and you will have created a road map for future success.

CHAPTER THREE

The Perfect Match

Once you have completed a hiring plan and know that you need to hire for a particular position or several positions, you can start identifying what skill sets are necessary in these roles. Through further identification and planning, you can find the perfect match.

Ponder this for a moment: Is there a correlation between finding your perfect *soul mate* and finding the perfect people to work for your company? We believe this correlation may exist, although *perfect* is hard to define. For our purposes, we will define *perfect* as top performers that bring value to your organization.

During this process, challenge any preconceived notions you may have about hiring and your company's current hiring processes. We want you to see through the eyes of a potential employee as they interview with your company.

By understanding the correlation of hiring as it relates to human relationships, like those in your personal life, you can develop stronger interviewing skills. In turn, those skills will allow you to ask the right questions during interviews. By asking the right questions, you will develop a stronger employee-employer relationship with your new hires starting on Day One.

The interviewing process is really not that different from the dating world as it relates to relationships. In the interview process, as the interviewer, you're generally looking for someone with passion, excitement, and common interests. Okay, we'll agree that you're probably not going to marry them! Still, many of the key attributes will be similar. As recruiters, many times we wonder, "Where's the passion?" or "What about the excitement level?" With a lack of emotion or interest between the parties, the hiring process can be unbelievably similar to a weathered relationship, fraught with boredom and indignation. It shouldn't be this way. It should be positive for both the potential candidate and the employer. And it can be!

"Every interaction with a candidate counts."

Rita Wright Gurian, Retired Healthcare Executive—Current Non-Profit & Professional Development Coach, thirty-plus years' hiring experience in Healthcare, Non-Profit

---

The Application Process

Applying to a job can be simple or complex. Some companies make applying for a job very easy with short online applications while others have more extensive, often complicated processes.

I am reminded of my daughter's best friend who just graduated from college and has been applying for jobs in her field of interest. She called me to find out how to get past the auto-responses. She has been filling out applications online and has received email responses that her resume has been received, but they all say, "Don't call us. We will call you if you make it."

Understandably, her excitement level since graduating and attempting to start her career has diminished. In fact, one of those companies to which she applied told her that she was one of many that made it to the next level. They asked her to fill out an application and told her that applications would open at 7 a.m. on a first-come, first-serve basis. She prepared her answers the night before, got up early and went online to apply enthusiastically at 7 a.m. to submit her information. Several months went by and she still didn't hear from the company and was not able to reach anyone by phone. We have all been there!

Keep this in mind as you interview. It might be a good idea to ask candidates you decide to interview about their experience applying to your company. A simple bank of questions may help improve your process. Often, getting feedback on your company's application process can be valuable in your ability to recruit top talent in the future. Auto-responses are a necessary evil in online applications; we use them in our recruiting business as well. But keep in mind that it can discourage top talent from applying. The future of recruiting may include machine learning and artificial intelligence, but, I believe that human interaction and decisions can never truly be replaced.

"Treat all with respect and enthusiasm. I want them to WANT the job."

Marc Waldman, VP Business Development, twenty years' hiring experience, Medical Device

When Does The Relationship Begin?

To find out more about when a relationship begins, we surveyed our contributing panel of hiring managers, asking, "When do you feel your relationship with a potential candidate / new hire begins? Pre-hire or Post-hire?" The results were informative—93% agree that the relationship begins pre-hire. This is important because a candidate is evaluating you and your company just as much as you are evaluating them throughout the hiring process. It is definitely a two-way street, and it should be.

From the initial contact forward, each interview should be the beginning of an interesting, if not revealing, relationship between an employer and a potential employee. Early in the process, there should be common ground established and open dialog between the parties. If there is not a genuine interest or excitement formed between the potential employer and the candidate, then why continue? Believe it or not, many times the recruitment process or relationship progresses simply because of corporate process and procedure. There is no definitive end-point established to end the candidacy. The candidate was never "on fire" or passionate about the position but simply met the basic criteria as set forth in a job description. Conversely, the hiring company brought on someone "lukewarm" because, for whatever reason, they thought that this candidate might be the best they could find. Later, maybe both parties realize that this may not be a match made in heaven. But by then it's too late. There is now a relationship between an employer and new employee that should never have been established. This is very similar to a romantic relationship again. We call it "settling": a person dates someone that they are not convinced is their soul mate.

Many things get in the way of our quest to hire the right person. Sometimes an organization's own protocol drowns the candidate in frivolous tasks before actually being on-boarded. Some of the issues around the hiring protocol are based upon process and procedure. Many in the HR world are concerned about all the legalities in the hiring process, which is justified. Still, other managers and directors are constantly under pressure to place individuals in roles in a timely manner. Finally, many managers are busy juggling the schedules of the interviewers, and executives and are faced with tough judgment calls.

Obviously, all of these are important areas, but we can surely see how they get in the way of connecting our expectations with a good candidate in a timely, efficient manner. Most hiring professionals realize that there are elements of the hiring process that must be uniform, and—for lack of a better description—mundane. Although the uniformity in process and procedure must exist in many organizations, the excitement, and passion in the hiring process must also be present.

Without a doubt, you should be a people pusher. No, we're not talking about you being a villainous manager pushing folks to their limits. We mean the kind of manager who fosters leaders by bringing people in and *pushing* for the right new hires, the right trainers, the best district managers, and so forth. When you hire the right employees for their respective roles, your job as their manager is to encourage them with a nudge of passion versus the traditional push for performance. Your new employee should *want* to do a great job based on their background and initiative. Their ability already exists, you simply must place them in the right role to foster their growth!

> **"...being transparent, candid, and honest sets the tone from the first interaction. It's important we both understand there are no hidden agendas and we are building our trust from day one. I don't want someone accepting an offer expecting something different than what they are signing up for."**
>
> *Matt Aultman, District Sales Manager, six years' hiring experience, Pharmaceutical Sales*

The relationships developed and cultivated during the interview and evaluation process should be of excitement and curiosity between the parties. Yes, the formalities, processes, evaluations, and background checks will all be in play, but fostering the potential of a new hire is incredible. This is the start of something new! So, if either party lacks passion or excitement, maybe the potential fit just isn't there.

Unfortunately, somewhere along the way, hiring has become more of a process instead of a pleasure. Getting back to the right person for the right job may be easier than you think if you apply these ideas.

> **"… you should be 'yourself' throughout the process. This is fair to both the candidate and yourself in ensuring a fit."**
>
> *David Eberson, Vice President Commercialization, Sales and Service, North America, twenty-five years' hiring experience, Medical Device and Pharmaceuticals*

Selecting the Right Person

Now that you have established a hiring plan and know who, what, when, where and why you need this position, let's start the process of selecting the right person for the job. To do this, think about the interview process a little differently. Consider it the start of a potential relationship—a relationship that begins the moment you look at the individual's resume or hear about them from another person.

Again, this initial contact may well resemble how people often meet in a romantic relationship. Similarities may include:

Meeting online –Initial Contact is made through technology. But rather than being matched on a dating site, the candidate has sent their resume via your company's website. You don't know anything about them, only what they have put on paper. When you meet a candidate through an online response, you mentally swipe *yes* or *no* based on limited information and gut instinct.

The blind date – This is a candidate referred to you through another party, possibly another employee, a recruiter, or someone outside of the organization. You have a little more background information with this scenario, so you may be a little bit more intrigued.

An Acquaintance – This is a candidate that you have met previously but do not know much about. For instance, the candidate might be someone you met at a trade show. They could also be a personal acquaintance that you know outside of your business that you feel might have the qualities to excel in a position.

A Relationship from the Past – You know this person because you have previously worked with them. Because of this, you may or may not be comfortable interviewing them.

The point of these previous examples is to help you understand that many candidates will see you in the same way. Have they heard of your company before? Or maybe it is like a blind date? If it is like a blind date, then you and the candidate will need to get to know one another, and that generally takes more interviews and time.

My husband, Randy, likes to give our daughter advice on dating. He thinks it is funny to tell her, "Marry for money, honey. Love will come later." She usually laughs and tells him that he is not that funny.

But isn't that what we do in hiring employees? We choose individuals to interview because we think their résumé fits a position, but at times, we don't consider if they will fit within our organization's culture. For this reason, it's important that we take time to talk about our organization and its strengths and weaknesses. No candidate is perfect, but neither is an organization. Fostering an open dialog about the role and the organization may help the candidate feel at ease and help them to understand more about the company and position. We can't always expect that "love will come later."

Identify the Pillars

A few years ago, my daughter received dating advice from a close friend. He said, "Decide what qualities you need to have in a potential person and don't date anyone who lacks those essential qualities." He was describing pillars. Pillars, the cornerstones that support a building from the ground up, that make it strong. In a potential mate, those pillars might be the same belief system, generosity, or overall character. But in a potential employee, that might be their education, experience, or skills.

My daughter's friend went on to say, "After you decide what the essentials are, stop wasting time on developing a relationship with someone that doesn't meet your essential qualifications."

Pretty good advice, don't you think?

The colloquial definition of a pillar might be "a person or thing regarded as reliably providing essential support." You're looking for this foundational individual who can add value to the organization through enhanced revenue to your team and provide a high level of support in other fashions.

You can probably think of several associates or people you know who are known as *pillars of the community*. In other words, people of respect, character, and value. For our purposes, the pillars are contained within a well-defined job description and may include the job title, the job qualifications, the necessary education, the key skill sets, and any other attributes necessary to carry out the job functions.

So how do you define "pillars" in a hiring situation? The first step is to define the pillars (AKA qualifications, experience, key skills, and attributes) required for the role you are filling. This can be done by developing a well-written job description.

> "Job descriptions are extremely helpful for the fact that a candidate knows exactly what they are up against with no surprises after they go through the onboarding process."
>
> *Todd Derickson, Director of Sales, twenty-plus years' hiring experience, Medical Device*

Job descriptions are often underrated, sometimes viewed as more paperwork to be stuffed in a personnel file and never looked at again. But I challenge you to look at a job description differently by realizing its value not only for the company but also for the employee.

> [Job descriptions] "...point you to specific competencies that a candidate will need to have to perform the role well. For example, a Regulatory Specialist with a job description describing compliance to regulations means we need someone who is not only detailed oriented but forward thinking in what regulations may be coming down the road."
>
> *Tracy Barry, Sr. HR Partner, fifteen-plus years' hiring experience, Medical Device, Pharmaceuticals, Financial Services, and Publishing*

A well-written job description can be an employee's road map. It can help them understand their role within the organization and your expectations. A job description should be one to two pages in length. It should include the title of the position, the supervisor, a short description of the company, a position summary, the position duties, the qualifications, education, and experience required, and any other additional key attributes. It is also good to add a statement that implies that the responsibilities and duties listed are intended to be general in nature and not intended to be an exhaustive list of all responsibilities, duties, and skills.

A job description can have a variety of uses. It should be used to assist in performance appraisals and answer questions like, "Does the person meet the qualifications and expectations?" If not, then a job description can assist a company during unfortunate events, such as an employee termination.

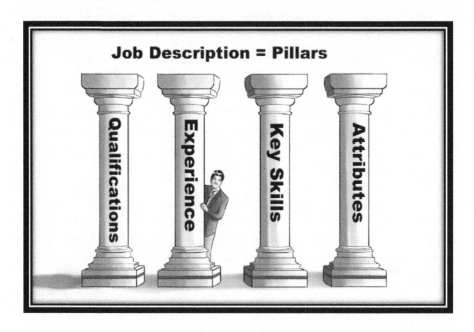

Compare this to your personal relationships. An appraisal system is like an anniversary. Anniversaries allow you to reflect on the past and plan for the future. One type of appraisal system focuses on the essential job functions and duties. It uses a weighted system, where each function or duty is given a percentage. Typically, the percentage assigned is based upon the percentage of time the employee will spend on the function.

For example, a salesperson might spend 70 percent of their time in the field closing business, 10 percent on inventory and 20 percent on reports. With this system, they are ranked on a scale of 0 to 10 for each job function, thereby providing a heavier weight to the job functions that are most important to the organization and to their role within it. We will discuss this more in Chapter 10.

> **[Job Descriptions] "...give both the hiring manager and candidate a common framework to discuss the open position."**
>
> *Mike DeMuth, VP Sales, fifteen years' hiring experience in Healthcare Information Technology*

The job description is vital to a successful employer-employee relationship. Funny enough, many of our personal relationships have unwritten job descriptions. Randy and I have been married for more than thirty years. Yes, he likes to say that we have been married "thirty-two years, in a row, without a break." But all kidding aside, we would not have lasted as a couple if we hadn't figured out who would do what within the marriage. I am very pleased to say that since we live and work together every day we share a lot of the household duties. Like one of your employees, we have our essential job functions and duties, and they are based upon our qualifications, key skills, attributes and experiences in life. After being married for this long, we have figured out what we do best. We both work diligently in our recruiting firm, but he is good at fixing things like computer hardware, the car and electronics, and he is also great at building things. Meanwhile, I am better at creating things, implementing new software, and of course, shopping. The point is that it works because we recognize our particular skill sets, the duties, and responsibilities, and we have assigned the right individual to do the job. The same is true with your company.

So now that you have designed a well-written job description, how do you find the right person to fill the role? We discussed earlier in this chapter that there were multiple ways for people to meet. Obviously, since we are recruiters, we feel that our role can be very helpful. Recruiters are matchmakers. We match the qualifications, experience, key skills, and attributes and locate interested individuals that meet those qualifications. We are also cheerleaders for both the company and the candidate. By assisting both, we become a mediator so that the two parties better understand each other. Ask any recruiter—we want our matches to work. There is nothing worse than placing an individual in a job where they are unhappy or putting the wrong candidate in a role for a client. As recruiters, we spend time getting to know our clients by asking questions about the organization's culture so that we place people in the right type of environment.

Finding the right candidate for our clients means understanding what qualifications and skills (or pillars) are important to the role. Prior to recruiting for our clients, we typically require a written job description. This is because we are convinced that the key to a successful hire is built upon these pillars, as it may lay the foundation for success. The time spent creating this document will be worth it. It will save you time, energy, and heartache in the long run.

Now let's turn to the selection process in more depth.

♨ CHAPTER FOUR

Interview with FIRE

Now that you have a written job description, you can move to the selection, screening, and interview phase of the hiring process.

In most companies today, it is typical to interview a candidate anywhere from three to five times before making them an offer. As recruiters, we are usually involved in setting up the first phone interview, the second face-to-face meeting—whether by video conference or in-person—and a third final interview for our clients. Prior to doing so, we do a thirty- to sixty-minute review of the person's résumé and talk with the candidates who, on paper, we feel look like a good match for the position. This is known as our pre-screen. With hundreds of résumé submissions for one position, the pre-screen is vital. It allows us to review each résumé for specific criteria in a timely manner to quickly identify potential candidates for a position. Selection is the most basic and important function of the hiring process. Although technology exists to assist with this function, I still believe nothing can replace human interaction and participation in the screening process.

Randy and I own a 280-acre ranch that has been in his family for over a century. We have raised cattle, which means we sometimes have to round them up. This process is referred to as a "cattle call". During a cattle call, we will typically round up a larger group of cattle from the herd and then release each cow one by one back into the field as we finish branding or vaccinating them. The process works well most times.

Some candidates also use the term "cattle call" when they are interviewing for a position along with many others; it is not a positive experience. When companies contact a large number of candidates to interview, candidates can potentially feel less important. After all, doesn't everyone want to feel special? We believe that if you want to ignite passion in a future employee, it starts with your first interaction. The candidate wants to feel that they were selected for an interview based on their background and the skills they can bring to the company. They do not want to feel like just one of many in your pool of potential candidates.

So how do you make each candidate feel special? One way is to not waste their time. No one wants to be called to an interview to find out later that their background or education was not a match for the position. Unfortunately, this situation happens all too often.

But what do you do if you have a large number of candidates you feel might be a good fit for an open position? You might start by sorting the résumé into three different piles. I had one manager that would put them into "A candidates," "B candidates," and "C candidates." He would start interviewing with the résumés of those he felt were "A candidates."

If you do find that you have a large number of people for the same position, perform a thirty-minute phone pre-screen to make your first selections. Then, if you still think you have too many candidates, just work your way through the selection process. It might take longer, but it is an important decision. Try not to let the candidates know they are part of a large group of people, even if they ask. If you want to see someone's passion for a job drop, tell them you are interviewing more than ten other people for the same position. To avoid this discussion, let them know why they were selected to interview and thank them for their time so that they feel the interest and time they invested was appreciated.

Preparation is also important. Prepare ahead of time for the pre-screen or first phone interview. By reviewing a candidate's résumé in advance, you will be able to ask appropriate questions and get to know each candidate better. As recruiters, we tell our candidates to prepare for the interview, but as the hiring manager, it is absolutely vital for you to prepare as well. Everyone likes to work with someone who is organized.

This is one of the things that attracted me to Randy when we first started dating—he would plan out our dates. I saw that early on, he wanted to impress me, and that made me more interested. By preparing in advance instead of just asking me what I wanted to do, he made me much more comfortable with him. The same is true of a potential candidate. By preparing questions ahead of time, you are respecting the candidate's time, and this will help you develop a better relationship with this potential employee.

Honesty is another important quality. During the pre-screening phone call, be honest with the candidate. If they do not meet the requirements for the position outlined in the job description, let them know. This provides them the time for an open discussion with you, allowing them to correct any misunderstandings or miscommunication. We have found that candidates would rather be told they are not moving forward than be left to wonder. No one likes to be the person who isn't called back and left wondering why. Timely follow-up will make your company (and you as a manager) stand out.

FIRE Interview Method©

Several years ago, we established a pre-screening tool that has served us well. Its simple structure and usability make it a perfect instrument to challenge and select candidates during the résumé review, pre-screening, and interview process. Known as the *FIRE Interview Method*, it outlines the key variables that we've found most employers agree upon when initially identifying talent.

The acronym FIRE represents four areas to consider functionality, integrity, results, and enthusiasm. These areas will help you to quickly select outstanding talent amongst hundreds of résumés. Identifying superior talent and sometimes eliminating candidates is an important function in the recruiting process. In today's environment, there is a plethora of good talent. Identifying the very best out of this pool is key to successfully developing your epic team.

Our job, as recruiters, is to find and recruit the best candidates for our clients. To do this, we talk to a lot of potential candidates and in doing so, cover the basic questions (past experience, education, compensation requirements, accomplishments, etc.) to find candidates that match the qualifications of the position.

The following examples will show you the criteria we utilize, some basic questions we ask during the prescreen process, and how the FIRE acronym can be developed specifically to meet your hiring needs.

Fire Interview Pre-Screen Criteria©

Functionality

- ✓ Candidate's key skills and abilities fit the job description's minimum requirements.

Integrity

- ✓ Explains past career moves or changes.
- ✓ Explains any gaps in the dates listed on resume.
- ✓ Provides a clear explanation and verification of employment history.

Results

- ✓ Able to present a concise snapshot of their career successes.
- ✓ Provide references that are able to verify results of past performance.
- ✓ Explains their career experiences and how they have learned to improve.
- ✓ Discuss any awards of achievements and the criteria around their successes.

Enthusiasm

- ✓ Candidate returns phone calls promptly.
- ✓ Fills out information quickly, without a reminder
- ✓ Sends a thank you note to interviewer.
- ✓ Follows-up as necessary.
- ✓ Displays a good overall attitude, communicates well and is cooperative.

FIRE Pre-screen Form

Name: _____   Date: _____

Email address: _____

FUNCTIONALITY

Current position: _____

Territory: _____Ability to travel: _____%

Duties: (products, customers): _____

Reason for Leaving: _____

Education: _____

INTEGRITY

Past Company: _____Reason for Leaving: _____

Past Company: _____Reason for Leaving: _____

Background check/driving record verification _____

Discuss any questionable areas on resume (such as employment gaps, changes in career):

RESULTS

Tell me some of your accomplishments:

1. _____

2. _____

3. _____

ENTHUSIASM

What are your professional goals for the next five years?

How available will you be for interviews during the next couple of weeks?

Presented to client(s): _____ (   ) Date: _____

The FIRE method is not just used for pre-screening candidates. It can help you develop questions to use on the first, second, or even third interview. For the purpose of recruitment, we use it in pre-screening. However, questions you develop that focus on its core traits (functionality, integrity, results, and enthusiasm) will benefit you throughout the interview and hiring process.

You will get a better understanding of each candidate starting with your first phone interview. This is the time to take notes and begin what we will refer to as the FIRE Interview Method. The FIRE Interview Method© is designed to refine the selection process of candidates. Using each of the key components within the tool is critical. The tool serves to help quickly differentiate and identify the abilities and qualifications of each candidate. To further understand FIRE, let's take a look at the individual areas:

Functionality

The "F" in FIRE stands for functionality. The term *functionality* means to serve a purpose well. Candidates should be able to serve a purpose well. Obviously, the individual's background is highly important. Do they have the core components for the position? Are they designed for the job? Is the individual suited to serve the purpose of this position well?

The candidate who cannot show functionality is at a great disadvantage. Many times these are intrinsic traits that can be difficult to teach. Improvement is possible, but an initial aptitude will show up in the interview. Functionality in dealing with the many situations that can and do occur should be high on your radar. These are traits that will help make members of the team successful. Reviewing a person's background helps the recruiter or hiring manager identify the key elements in the functionality of the potential candidate.

Included in this area are the tasks that are expected of the individual when they assume the role. These are generally outlined in the job description but may be implied by generalized statements such as, "and other roles as the organization may require." Clearly, hiring personnel will look at a candidate's background relative to their key skills and abilities to meet the demands of the position. Often hiring managers will look beyond a job description. Yes, the candidate meets those basic requirements, but as an example they also have experience in public speaking, a potential future perk to the organization. Skill sets and abilities can and do vary widely amongst a group of viable candidates.

Before you as a manager can apply this part of the model, you and your organization must carefully review what both the essential and marginal job functions may include. In the sales world, this might be abilities like learning products, analyzing data, understanding a sales territory, general ability to organize, and communication with customers, just to cite a few. Marginal job responsibilities might include those qualifications that are *nice to have* but are not mandatory. In setting up new positions, many professionals create a worksheet outlining the actual needs of the position while also identifying those traits or skills necessary for the successful candidate. This worksheet can later be used in a comparative analysis between evaluating a potential candidate's skill sets against the requirements of the job. If you can't make a positive assessment of the candidate in the functionality portion of the FIRE formula, then it's not wise to move on to the next step.

Integrity

The "I" in FIRE represents integrity. This is the personal credo or mantra a candidate may exhibit; it may show up in a review of their background as well as throughout the interview process. The sometimes dreaded, all-encompassing question, "Tell me about yourself" will elicit some very revealing answers. These questions often reflect upon a candidate's overall character. This is also an area of the interview process that includes various situational or behavioral questions such as, "Tell me about a time when you had to…" This type of question helps the interviewer understand how a candidate will think through a process or procedure.

Additionally, in their response the candidate may display a lapse in judgment or common sense. In extreme cases, a candidate may cite an example that causes the interviewer to question the candidate's ethics. Ultimately, this is a red flag.

This happened during an interview with a potential candidate I worked with. When asked if they knew anyone in a certain department in a hospital, they quickly responded, "Yes." Unfortunately, when they were asked who, they were unable to come up with a name. This could be a red flag. Although the candidate most likely responded "yes" to the question because they wanted the position, ultimately the manager did not move forward with them because their response was not substantiated.

Character is more than the latest word of the week plastered on the local school billboard. As a student or citizen, we drive by and identify with the word or phrase, but some do not really practice character awareness, or even more importantly, development. Parents, teachers, and churches speak to the issues of character, but ultimately, it is the individual's responsibility to work on being a person of impeccable character.

By definition, character is the aggregate of features and traits that form the individual nature of a human being. It's the moral or ethical quality of an individual. In its strictest sense, character is who we are and it's reflected in our behavior. Many times, this is the key trait a manager will look for in a candidate before they move on to their abilities. As a manager, you want to know that an employee will choose the ethically right road to avoid future embarrassment, loss of business, criticism, or even potential liability. We've heard the phrase that he or she is "a man or woman of fine, honorable character." Character deals with the qualities of honesty, courage, and the like; it deals with integrity, which is adhering to being moral and ethical. So when a manager evaluates an individual, they take into account a person's reputation and will consider their qualities or peculiarities.

Most of us understand that building character is a road, not a destination. We all deal with making good (and sometimes not so good) decisions every day. Our experiences and awareness of good versus bad help us make decisions. As a hiring manager, you have undoubtedly used behavioral-type questions to help bring out answers that will provide a reflection into a candidate's past and provide an insight into their future actions. Understandably, everyone has made mistakes or has been influenced in a not-so-positive way by friends or family members, but it's what these lessons teach us that make them a learning, growing experience. When evaluating candidates, it's possible to keep an open mind while still maintaining a critical view of the person before you. At the end of the interview day, evaluate each candidate as a total package, not a bank of individual responses.

Sometimes we get hung up on an individual response to a seemingly less-important question and don't consider the stellar responses to our other questions. Keep an open mind and, if one response to a question was critical in determining your attitude to the candidate, come back to that question in a successive interview. You may receive a response that effectively eliminates a candidate, but don't let it remove the candidate if they are the best person for the job in all other areas!

There are many questions that will help you gain insight into a candidate's integrity. For example, questioning a candidate about their career moves can be helpful. You can better understand a person's career goals by asking how often they have switched jobs and why they made those moves. Would they leave your organization for a better opportunity or as a "step up?" These are all areas that show how the person thinks and operates. Sometimes, you have to listen to your gut. In our survey, 86% of our hiring manager contributors said they have hired or not hired someone based upon their gut reaction. When asked how the situation worked out, most felt that their intuition did not steer them wrong.

> **"My *gut* reaction is only one of many things I take into account, but it can be important in determining the *fit*."**
>
> *Greg Burris, President & CEO, United Way of the Ozarks, thirty years' hiring experience, Non-profit, Higher Education, City Government- former City Manager for the City of Springfield, Missouri*

The final check for integrity would be to perform a background check and drug screen. This will help you know if your gut instincts are correct. Reference checks offer some insight into an individual's background and abilities, but they are not conclusive, as many companies do not give out information other than dates of employment and rehire status.

> **"...A good CV can only provide you with enough basic information on the candidate and their qualifying skills. The "gut" reaction is what you experience and understand from past hires (success or failures) and what your feeling is for this candidate and the role they will play in the organization. Example: I hired an individual that had less qualifications and experience than all other candidates based on a "gut" reaction. That individual was one of my best hires to date. (They are now a VP of Sales!)"**
>
> *Steve Ford, Senior Manager of New Market Development, twenty-plus years' hiring experience, Pharmaceuticals, Capital Equipment, and Medical Device*

Results

We are strong believers that past performance is a good indicator of future results. So, the "R" in FIRE represents results. An exceptional candidate should be able to present, verify, and document their past successes. So why not ask if they have proof of the accomplishments listed on their résumé on your first phone interview? This should not be limited to sales or other performance numbers, but also projects, special awards, raises based on performance, bonuses, and any other documented accolades. If you ask this question upfront, it may save you valuable time by helping you determine if the individual tracks and cares about their own performance.

So many times as sales recruiters, we deal with candidates who tell us that they sold a product. However, their résumé doesn't tell us how well they sold it. Obviously, in the sales world, prospective employers want to know your sales ability and how you can grow sales in their environment. Results are just one quantifiable measure of performance. If candidate A sold 500 products and candidate B sold 2,000, then candidate B's numbers appear superior if all other variables are equal (which is sometimes a big assumption). At any rate, including the results as a part of the evaluation process is important. Similar to Newton's Law of Motion—an object in motion tends to stay in motion unless acted upon by another force—so goes the professional sales representative. Long-term success in any role seems to be based upon a sustained momentum over time.

Some entry-level positions can be available to candidates with limited experience. This can make evaluating for results a bit more difficult since the candidate may not have held a similar position. The interviewer may feel they are taking a chance if they hire an individual without a proven track record. However, there are still areas to consider. When evaluating an entry-level candidate, review their experiences in high school or college to determine if they excelled. You can do this by reviewing their grade point average, any leadership positions they may have held or additional extracurricular activities. Successful people seem to stay successful and relish personal and professional recognition.

Enthusiasm

Finally, we're up to the "E" in FIRE. Many times we have heard that the "candidate lacked enthusiasm... They just don't seem to be that excited about the opportunity." This can be heartbreaking for the candidate who simply has trouble displaying their passion. Most interviewers can tolerate, maybe appreciate, a candidate being a little over the top rather than too reserved.

To find out more, we asked our contributing panel of hiring managers, "Would you rather hire someone with all the necessary skills for the position but who lacks passion or someone with fewer skills that is more passionate? 73% said they would rather hire someone with fewer skills who is more passionate; while 27% agreed that although passion was very important, they also felt that in some positions skills and experience can determine the choice.

Throughout the interview process, look for candidates that seem passionate. Think about your own purchase experiences. Whether on a big-ticket or everyday purchases, customers enjoy interacting with sales personnel who are cordial, polite, attentive, smiling, and engaged. People who are engaged are typically passionate and it shows. You might think this is a given, but it's not. We tend to look at candidates in terms of a more objective criteria first. A review of their résumé and the accolades presented right before us on paper, not so much an analysis of the personality of the person sitting in front of us.

Still, the information on their résumé is critically important. It should give us a portrait of what they've done and specifically how well they've done it. However, we need to dive deeper into what inspires this person. You will need a full understanding of the potential new hire, one that will include their overall satisfaction in their career thus far. As we know, great past performance can generally predict future performance, but not always. We know there is no perfect candidate, right? But there also is no perfect school, church, job, husband, or wife. In fact, we are surrounded by imperfect things. This is why we look at enthusiasm and passion as a key ingredient into a person's strong performance and potential lengthy tenure.

How do we get to some of this subjectivity and emotion? I am reminded of a candidate who told us post-interview that he thought the interviewer might know him better than he knew himself! Obviously, that interviewer knew how to elicit information from the candidate that they might not have intended to share. This gave the interviewer a more comprehensive view of the individual. That sort of thing can take a thirty-minute interview into a two-hour experience. We've seen this occur many times in a form we call the *detective* interview style. The interviewer circles back around and asks, "Just one more question." That question and the subsequent answers potentially lead to other questions and clarifications, really revealing the personality and motivations of an individual, which help you decide if they are a fit for your organizational culture and team.

As sales recruiters, nothing hurts us so badly as when we ask a candidate if they "closed" (or asked) for the position, and they either respond by saying "I didn't get the chance," or "There was not an appropriate time," or simply, "No, I didn't." This is heart-breaking, since it is such an integral part of almost all sales calls. You know as a hiring manager, an interview is nothing more than a sales call set up for that candidate to showcase and sell themselves to you as the best person for the position. Although many positions are not sales-related, it is almost always appropriate to ask about the next step.

The enthusiasm part of the *HIRE with FIRE* formula really reaches a high point at end of the interview. The true excitement of what has happened to this point in the interview process effectively ends with the interviewer asking for the job. Hopefully, this is a right (somewhat of an obligation) that the interviewee has earned and should not be assumed or taken for granted. It is the single reason they have been meeting with you—to close the deal and get the job!

Let's recap before the next step, which is developing interviewing questions around the key components of FIRE.

HIRE with FIRE Interview Process©

Functionality

Functionality evaluates the candidate's education, qualifications, and key skills/abilities to do the job. A comparison between the candidate and job description can be helpful. Do they have the core components for the position?

Integrity

Integrity evaluates the candidate's overall character. This can be evaluated by asking situational or behavioral questions, such as "Tell me about a time when you had to.." or "How would you handle..." Background checks are a vital part of evaluating a candidate's integrity.

Results

Results evaluates a candidate's past accomplishments. It is based on the theory that past performance is a good indicator of future results.
An exceptional candidate should be able to present, verify and document their past successes.

Enthusiasm

Enthusiasm evaluates the candidate's level of passion and interest displayed throughout the interview process. Is the candidate prepared for the interview? Are they engaged in your discussions? Did they send a thank you note? Do they seem engaged in their career?

Develop Ten Questions

The questions you ask during the interview process can have an impact on your hiring decision and your relationship with the candidate. Vague questions can often produce unclear answers, while direct, well-thought-out questions may enable you to get the answers you need quickly to make a good hiring decision. We encourage you to develop ten questions around the four components of FIRE.

To do this, first ask three questions in relation to the candidate's functionality, current job functions, and how it pertains to this role. Then, ask three questions that will help you determine their integrity by using situational or behavioral interview questions designed toward evaluating ethical behavior. Next, ask them three questions about their accomplishments and their past results. Finally, ask a question that will help you assess their level of enthusiasm. After asking these questions, you should get a feel for their fit for the position.

There are an infinite number of interview questions out there, and obviously, many questions you should also avoid asking. Even though we want you to consider the relationship aspect of interviewing, your questioning should never be on a personal basis. Questions such as the year they graduated high school (or college), if they are married, how many children they have or questions regarding their heritage are just a few to avoid, as they may be discriminatory in nature. Keep your interactions and questions business-related and not personal. Candidates might bring up some of their personal information during an interview on their own, but it is never appropriate to ask for this information.

Below is a short example of some questions you might use when interviewing candidates with the FIRE method. I would encourage you to make a list of your ten questions, similar to this one, to help you implement the FIRE methodology into your current interviewing style.

Functionality Question Examples:

1. What is your understanding of the job for which you are applying?

2. Tell me about your last performance review. In which areas were you most disappointed?

3. What qualifies you for this job?

Additional questions may include:

What do you know about our company?

What is your greatest strength? What is your greatest weakness?

Integrity Question Examples

1. What would you do if you caught a colleague lying?

2. Tell me about a stressful event at work and how you handled it.

3. When you say you are going to do something, do you always do it? Can you describe a time when you were not able to complete a task and how you handled that situation?

Result Based Question Examples

1. What achievement in your career are you most proud?

2. How much direction and feedback do you need in order to excel?

3. How have you added value to your current employer over the last year?

Additional questions may include:

If your coworkers were sitting here, what would they say about you and your work?

Enthusiasm Question Examples:

1. On a scale of 1 to 10 how excited are you about this position?

Additional questions may include:

What motivates or encourages you to do a good job?

Many books have been written regarding questions that can be used for interviewing purposes. There are several types of interviewing questions used by companies today: behavioral, situational, competency-based, problem-solving, and a few others. Some companies even use brainteaser questions to see if the candidate can be creative. For the purpose of this book, we will leave it to the specialists in your field to suggest which specific interview questions you should ask. With many questions available, it is important to focus on those that will make the biggest impact on your team and organization. To do this, you will need to be organized and strategic with your approach to questioning. Spend time developing interview questions that will give insight into how a potential candidate will perform on the job. This is essential, and you would be surprised how many managers just "wing it." This lack of preparation causes the interview to mainly be a "get to know" you session. Unfortunately, without appropriate questions the manager is forced to base their hiring decision on their "gut reaction." Interview preparation may be the biggest secret to a successful hire, and yet, it is not prioritized by most hiring managers.

When you develop specific questions that are well thought out, you have a foundation for your hiring decision. Also, when the same questions are asked of all candidates, it levels the playing field and will give you a better view of which candidates truly stand out. This makes the selection process much easier. By basing these questions on the *pillars* discussed in chapter three, you will form a firm foundation with your next hire. You wouldn't marry an individual without asking them quite a few questions while you are dating. The same goes for hiring. Don't hire anyone without a thorough interview process.

You will benefit from creating a bank of questions that you can use for specific positions. One size does not fit all, but these questions will help you organize as much as 75 percent of your interview format; the rest must be individualized to that specific job. In the medical sales world, in which we specialize, we attempt to ask questions that will ultimately determine if the candidate can sell. For years, we have successfully identified top talent based upon a candidate's background, their career preparation, and their past experience. Technical questions based upon a candidate's competency, such as "How would you approach this...?" are highly appropriate. Again, an open-ended question is always preferred so you can assess a candidate's thoughtful response.

A candidate's past performance needs to be documented, but it is even more important to make sure their competency-based answers match their documented performance. This acts as a cross-check. Individual performance must be ascertained and validated.

So, back to our goal of asking questions that will not discourage top talent. A thoughtful approach with questions that are directly relevant to performance should never offend or discourage a professional. If they are intimidated or mildly offended by these validations, it's a good idea to ask for further clarification or validation. Their successes should be a point of pride and honor, something they are ready, willing, and able to validate and discuss.

So, position maybe ten questions for each of your prospects after a careful review of their résumé. You may not need to hold fast to that direction, however, since ten questions and follow-ups will probably be more than you can ask in the allotted time. We would encourage starting with those questions that will provide you the most relevant view into what would make that person successful in your organizational environment. These, hopefully, provide you with attributes for your overall assessment of their potential success.

Additionally, opening with the open-ended question of, "Tell me a little about yourself" serves as an icebreaker and determines if the candidate can be clear and concise in their answers. If they start "chasing rabbits" too early in the interview, how could they maintain focus and clarity with your prospects and customers? A rambling employee could result in a lost sale or an unhappy customer.

I like questions that ask about the prospective company. This shows the ability of the candidate to research and serve back the information. "What do you know about our company?" Again, you're not looking for every intimate detail, just a well-thought-out concise explanation or overview of the goods or services offered. You might include some information relative to the company's public culture and their thoughts about that image. This is a check of the candidate's true interest. A solid response to this question should be required, and it is definitely fair game. How can a candidate be interested in working for your company without a base-line knowledge of its products, services, or market? This also should provide you a transition to the next question: "Why do you want to work here at XYZ Corporation?" This question, or one like it, will reveal if they have the background and desire to be on your team.

Once they've proven they have knowledge and background relative to your organization, let's look back at the candidate. How about: "If your coworkers were sitting here, what would they candidly say about you and your work?" Hopefully, this question won't make them flinch. Of course, you are looking for someone who can do the job, but you don't want a new hire who may alienate others in the process. We have all seen those who don't abide by the adage that "no man is an island." Some want to reside on that island! As a manager, you're quite aware that your job is to build a cohesive team, not to knowingly set up a dysfunctional group.

Candidates expect the question, "What is your greatest strength?" and "What is your greatest weakness?" Let's ask those for a couple of reasons. First, they're not easy questions, and secondly, they're hard to hit out of the park. These will give you an idea of their honesty and their ability to express themselves. They can't be too great or too weak. If they claim "no weaknesses," they're either lying or disconnected. If they are a superhero, then they will need to demonstrate those superpowers! Put on the cape!

One interesting question that gets right to character and truthfulness is "What motivates or encourages you to do a good job?" Look for solid, character-driven responses, not simply money, although we know that can and maybe should be a major driver. Many will look for recognition, awards, pride, or to be acknowledged and appreciated. Of course, there are a host of intangibles to be proud of from past performance. Additional questions related to a person's motivations or professional interests are also good to use to establish character. We once had a sales manager ask each candidate, "Why are you interested in this particular position?" Unfortunately, we had one candidate who answered that they "needed something to motivate them to get out of bed in the morning." No kidding! Unsurprisingly, that particular candidate did not move forward in the interview process.

The whole purpose of this discussion is to get you thinking about the type and number of questions you will be asking your candidates. Remember, we don't want to scare off our qualified candidates by asking questions that have little meaning to either party. All parties want a great discussion about how the candidate can benefit the organization, and in turn, how the qualified candidate can become a valued team member, making a positive difference to both their situation and the company's bottom line.

If you have carefully screened your résumés and conducted telephone interviews, you should have a good idea of what you are looking for in a new team member. This being said, most of the other questions will go by the wayside, and you will be laser-focused on those top several candidates anyway. Interestingly, ten well-thought-out questions will provide much more information than generic questions since they naturally beg for more information.

 Hopefully, your questions will allow you to determine who you are interested in moving forward in the interview process. You may begin to focus on one or two candidates whom you feel are the best match for your company and the position. During this time, it is still extremely important to express your interest in the candidate. One way to do this is to keep the interview process moving. As a manager, you have multiple obligations, and hiring is just one of them. Your time might be very constrained, but remember, just like in a dating relationship, you must keep communication flowing with your potential candidates. After a date, each person may wait for a call, text, or email to see if there is still interest from the other party. The situation is similar for a candidate who has invested their time in an interview. A simple acknowledgment of the candidate's time, through a phone call or email, will make all the difference in their enthusiasm and interest moving forward.

Using the components of FIRE will help you find a stand-out candidate more easily. Hiring can be difficult if you are following your gut reaction without specific direction. So instead of just using your gut, rank each candidate in the four FIRE areas. After you do, the right individual should stand out to you.

CHAPTER FIVE

The Elements of FIRE

Fire can be a scary word, invoking images of destruction. However, fire is not always bad. Although it causes destruction, it also refines and sterilizes many things. It helps us dispose of items we no longer need and provides us with heat, comfort, and serenity.

In more modern times, the word *fire* can describe someone that is passionate or angry, such as "Did you see the fire in his eyes?" When someone does something consistently well, we might say that they are "on fire." When we go through some of life's trials, then we might say we are being "put through the fire." People also say they are "under fire" at work or "were fired" when they have lost their job.

However, let's take a minute and imagine that the year is 1858. The event is the Nevada Silver Rush.[2] Dirt-covered miners are picking away at the tough rock walls of a dimly lit mine, ready to give up hope since there's no sign of desirable metal. Despite their doubts, they continue to hack away at the walls. Suddenly, a piece of silver chips off. The miner picks up the treasure and the rush for silver begins.

However, to be created into something usable, silver must be melted in a fire at 1,763 degrees Fahrenheit. In fact, without fire, silver—as

---

[2] Alden, Andrew, 2019. *The Nevada Silver Rush,* January 27. Accessed 09 20, 2019. https://www.thoughtco.com/nevada-silver-rush-1440699

well as many other fine metals—would not be of much value. What if we didn't have fire to refine these precious metals? It is our hope that if you use the FIRE components discussed in Chapter Four, it will refine the candidate selection and interview process for you.

Fire has been the topic of many stories over the course of history, maybe even as far back as a million years ago.[3] There have been entire cities destroyed or damaged by fire. My mother was born in Stuttgart, Germany, and grew up during World War II. She would tell me stories about her mother, father, and sisters running into underground bunkers during the bombings. She talked about the destruction and how the buildings would blaze with fire. She grew accustomed to seeing the destruction from fire; in fact, so much so that she and another boy her age would run into these burning buildings to retrieve important items for families. They both received a war merit medal from the German government for their efforts. I still have hers today. Even as a young child, she knew how fire could impact lives.

The Elements: Heat, Fuel, and Oxygen

You might ask why we chose the word *fire* as our acronym. There are lots of words we could have used. However, this particular word has a great significance. When a fire starts, change takes place. The item that is ignited no longer is the same. So, for the purpose of this book, we will be discussing the word *fire* in the sense of the change that can occur within your organization. Fire can also mean passion. We are all looking for candidates that are "on fire" for their job—those employees who are enthusiastic, easy to manage and that get the job

---

[3]. Cohen, Jennie (2012) Human Ancestors Tamed Fire Earlier Than Thought - Campfire remains from a South African cave suggest fire control by early humans dates back 1 million years. Accessed July 8, 2019 through https://www.history.com/news/human-ancestors-tamed-fire-earlier-than-thought.

done. You may have some of these individuals already on your team. They are your top performers. So how do you get a whole team full of people with these characteristics? Let's start by discussing the basic concepts about the creation of fire to gain a clearer understanding of what motivates people, then move forward.

In order for fire to start, there must first be an initial spark. Whether manmade or created by some type of natural disaster, certain conditions need to be in place for fire to occur. These conditions are known as the elements of fire—heat, fuel and an oxidizing agent (typically oxygen). These three elements must be present in the right mixture for fire to occur.

Similarly, we believe there are necessary elements for an employee-employer relationship to be successful. Like the elements necessary to start an actual fire, each trait in our FIRE acronym (functionality, integrity, results, and enthusiasm) must exist for there to be a success. Remember you are applying this method to find the very best match for your next great hire.

Look at it this way—an employee's functionality and integrity are the "heat" of the job. This includes their overall personality, competence, and integrity. It is the basis for their ability to perform their work.

Next, we evaluate their results or past accomplishments to see if they are a *results-oriented* individual. If they lack in this area, they may not complete the work you assign; in other words, they don't possess the necessary element of "fuel" that creates fire. This can also be caused by a lack of focus or poor organizational skills.

Lastly in FIRE, we evaluate their level of enthusiasm. Without enthusiasm, or—using our example—*oxygen*, an employee may not excel or do good work in the future. When we speak of someone "on fire," it is truly an enthusiastic person who is passionate about what they do.

Just like in an actual fire, each element in FIRE (functionality, integrity, results-oriented, and enthusiasm) must be present and is important to evaluate in each candidate. That is why screening is vital.

FIRE will help you identify and hire ideal candidates who will produce results for your organization, but let's not forget you, the hiring manager. Where do you fit into all of this? Well, the same elements are necessary. As the hiring manager, you will need keen management skills. Managing people is the focal point of your position. These skills are not something you are born with—they are acquired. Management skills should never be assumed. It is unfortunate that many times we promote people into supervisory roles and do not offer them any management training; potentially we are doing them a disservice.

You may have made an assumption that because a person was successful as an individual contributor that they will also be successful in leading a team. Maybe this stems from that fact that the employee has demonstrated three of the four elements of the FIRE acronym. Perhaps they have great integrity, they are result-oriented, and they are enthusiastic, so you make the assumption that they will be functional in a managerial role if you promote them. The point is, if we promote someone who lacks the functionality (key skills and abilities) necessary to do the job (i.e. managerial training), we could be setting them up for failure. That, in turn, can set up the company for lost revenue, damaged morale, potential legal disputes, EEOC compliance issues…the list goes on.

So, let's talk about you. Have you been through any management training? Are you comfortable supervising people, coaching your team, selecting candidates, interviewing and hiring people? If not, it might also benefit you to take management courses to help you feel more comfortable in your role. Ask if your organization offers tuition reimbursement.

The FIRE method has been developed and polished for many years. It represents more than 20 years in the development phase and is the culmination of results from thousands of interviews. Our methodologies have been used as a best practice by our team of recruiters, allowing uniformity, assisting compliance, and most importantly, finding the best fits between organizations and their employees. The goal is to create passionate and productive employees that are engaged. In order to create passion in others, you will need to establish great relationships first. Before we move to the next chapter, let's quickly define relationship-driven interviewing and the benefits it provides you and your company.

Relationship-Driven Interviewing

Relationship-driven managers are empathetic and enjoy empowering people. To define relationship-driven interviewing, let's look at both words a bit more closely. A relationship is defined as "the way in which two or more people, groups, countries, etc., talk to, behave toward, and deal with each other."[4] And interviewing is "a formal consultation usually to evaluate qualifications (as of a prospective student or employee)."[5]

If we combine these two definitions, relationship interviewing could be defined as, "how you behave or deal with someone when you formally meet to evaluate their qualifications." If we start to view interviewing as a human interaction, we can quickly see that it is the start of a potential working relationship. Beyond process and procedure, interviewing might actually make one of the biggest impacts on your company.

Relationship interviewing is the process of creating a positive relationship with each candidate, not just the candidates you hire. By creating a positive candidate experience, you will enhance your

---

[4] Merriam Webster. Accessed July 8, 2019. https://www.merriam-webster.com/dictionary/relationship.

[5] Merriam Webster. Accessed July 8, 2019 through https://www.merriam-webster.com/dictionary/interviewing.

employer brand and make employee recruitment easy. Top talent will want to work for your company.

How do you create a positive experience with the people you interview? It's not always easy. Over the next few chapters, we will compare the feelings that a candidate may have when going through the interview process to those feelings that occur during romantic dating relationships. Starting with Chapter Six, we will begin by discussing your first face-to-face meeting, which is comparable to a first date, because that's where the relationship really begins.

CHAPTER SIX

Relationships Begin on the First "Date"

Long, long ago in a place far away, there once was a very distinguished manager who was searching for his next great hire. He had spent time diligently planning *the who, what, when, where, and why* he needed for this position. He knew what skills the person needed in order to be successful and had written the duties of the job on a scroll. The manager then searched high and low to find suitable candidates to fill the position in his kingdom. He selected only the most qualified candidates to interview and sent them a royal Outlook® invitation to meet with him in the kingdom. They arrived on time to meet with him and so the story goes... Will he find his great hire? Only time will tell!

We know it's not a fairy tale world, but you too are a very distinguished manager looking to hire the right person for your kingdom. Hopefully, before you meet with any potential candidates, you have reviewed their résumé, pre-screened them, and selected the candidates you feel are the very best to interview. You think you might have a match, or it at least looks that way. You have spoken with them over the phone, asking pre-qualifying questions. They seem interested in your company and so you ask them to meet with you. Sound familiar? Yes, this is very much like asking someone out on a date, except this is a business meeting, and of course, there is a professional distance. You spend some time getting to know them, and then you decide if the relationship will work and if you will move them to the next step.

The Initial Interaction

Outside of the selection process, your role as a manager starts with the very first time you meet with or interact with the candidate either by phone or in-person. During this initial interaction, you will begin to evaluate the candidate; don't forget, the candidate is evaluating you and your organization, too. Hopefully, both parties have done a little research on one another prior to the initial meeting.

The initial interaction with this individual is incredibly important. Throughout the interview process, we are always amazed at how quickly relationships can develop and where they can take a candidate in the interview process. That is why preparing for this interaction is critical. Many interviewers do not take this interaction seriously, and it damages the company and their credibility with the candidate. Not only should you be prepared, but make sure you meet the candidate in a quiet, professional environment. There is nothing worse than meeting in a crowded restaurant and being unable to hear one another. Environmental distractions will not allow you to see a candidate's full potential and will leave them with a poor first impression of you and your company.

The organization of the interview format and the physical surroundings are important to both you and your prospects. You want to create a business environment, but also one that fosters a welcoming impression. A small conference room either at your office or a hotel works very well. Make sure the office staff or the hotel staff is aware that you are interviewing. Your office staff should be prepared with candidate names and the specific location of the interview within the complex. Nothing welcomes your candidates (don't forget, they are your guests) like a warm smile and greeting from a receptionist. Keep the receptionist advised of any delays or other updates. A few strategically placed items in the interview area, such as products or promotional material, may add a nice touch.

In addition, it's a nice gesture to welcome them by offering bagels or donuts and a cup of coffee. Meeting the prospect in the reception area is another plus. You will be able to interact with them in more informal surroundings and also make light conversation on the way to the interview suite or office. This will hopefully put them more at ease. Virtually everyone is nervous in the interview setting so do what you can to alleviate the candidates' anxiety. Why not meet around a more informal table, not face-to-face at a desk? Ultra-formal settings cause many to withdraw and not divulge enough information. You are trying to elicit as much relevant information as possible, so make it easy. While informality may encourage an individual to talk too much, you may get a clearer view of your candidate.

Once you've greeted one another with a firm handshake, it's time to get down to business. It's a really good idea to provide a personal background of yourself and your role with the company, a brief history of the organization, and an overview of the position itself. The candidate should be able to further the discussion about the company and the position based on their own research, so there is no need to go into great detail. By this point, you should have thoroughly reviewed your thoughts on the position and narrowed it down to the most relevant questions for your top prospects. You will probe the candidate not only to hear first-level responses but also quiz them on those areas that may require further clarifications. With an ideal atmosphere, you have them at ease; the interviews should just be a realistic discussion between business professionals. Remember, closed-ended questions are easy, but an open-ended question will reveal the true background and information. Most yes or no questions provide little value as to how a candidate will react in the role. Simply asking questions with *why* or *how* or *tell me* can get the ball rolling. The interviewee should be talking at least 75 percent of the time. The candidate should not be reluctant to talk. It's okay if they are a little nervous, but this is the beginning of their time to shine. From their dialogue, the interview can get a solid feel for the candidate's ability to express themselves in an intelligent and coherent manner. It's important for the candidate to take command of this part of the interview and show not only their abilities, but also interest in the opportunity.

You should have the candidate's résumé in front of you. You can ask specifics based upon their claims since they need to substantiate these claims to your satisfaction. In sales, questions such as, "Tell me how you were able to achieve your President's Club victory last year?" work well since you want them to perform similarly for your sales team if hired. After they've satisfactorily answered this question, take it to the next level. "What were the criteria for meeting that goal?" This second-level question makes them qualify their answer, such as providing a ranking, dollar amount of sales, or a market share percentage among possible other *gates*. These open-ended questions should elicit not only the significance of what they accomplished but also how they did it. So you can start with a seemingly informal question about one of their victories and really get a feel for their analytical skills, as well. This style of questioning avoids intimidation and comes across as genuine caring.

A great first impression can establish a connection between the interviewee and interviewer, creating a bond that may result in a lifetime friendship. For the relationship to gel, there must be content and connections that bring together common backgrounds and interests, either business or personal. Interesting enough, it's like love at first sight. For some reason, you connect with the individual and quickly feel confident in their abilities.

> **"Good communication helps to establish rapport. The hiring manager is the initial 'first impression' that a candidate has for a company."**
>
> *Reggie Steward, Regional Sales Director, two years' hiring experience, Medical Sales*

Failure to Bond

While great relationship-building can be successful, failure to bond can be devastating, even if the candidate has the perfect résumé. Everything is there: education, performance, skill sets, and work experience. This should be a great prospect! However, what happens next in the initial interview certainly doesn't match what's on paper. The candidate might show up late, exhibit a real or perceived lack of enthusiasm, or dress in unkempt attire. Whatever the case may be, they are successful in making an impression—the impression is just not the one that the candidate wished to make. Many times, the distracters, which are the small negative elements of the candidate's performance during the interview, can compound themselves and become significant concerns.

Unfortunately, not understanding the gravity of their failing interview, a candidate does not possess the ability or ammunition to quickly turn their image around. As you can imagine, this strongly and negatively impacts their chances of establishing a strong initial relationship, which many times will preclude them from moving on in the hiring process. This early relationship, or lack thereof, should not be confused with a good first impression, because it is truly different. Let us explain...

Picture yourself on the beach, your toes in the sand. Now, throw out a pebble into the water as far as you can. What happened? A small *kerplunk* with surrounding ripples emanating from the point of impact? That's a first impression. The longevity may be short-lived and a great candidate wants more. They position themselves for the high tide, a mini tsunami per se, to carry them to stardom with the interviewer and their future employer. The great candidate knows that the tide is coming, and there will be a group of opposing candidates that are working to maintain their own initial momentum by researching the company, the people, the business plan, growth, market share, and any number of other variables or pieces of data. The stellar candidate knows they will need to be much more than a forgettable, faint splash in the ocean—they must make bigger waves to propel themselves on to the next level.

As we all know, developing and maintaining great relationships is important in establishing and furthering one's career. We will leave most of that discussion to the plethora of networking books on your bookshelf. However, what we do need to discuss is the management of the developing relations within the interview process between you (the interviewer) and the candidate. This becomes a bit more complicated.

If it's possible, planning the interactions early is very helpful. Many candidates will be alerted by an organization's HR department that they will be screened or pre-screened. At the pre-screening level, the goal is to establish the candidate's ability to do whatever is expected within the scope of the advertised position. Early in the process, the interviewer (screener) wants to establish that the candidate at least possesses the minimum criteria, skills, and credentials to move them to the next levels. To establish this early relationship, screeners look for one key ingredient: *excitement*. More often than not, failure to connect at this level comes from a sense of complacency or lack of energy. As recruiters, we often hear, "I just didn't feel like John Doe was excited about the opportunity.... He hadn't even visited the website."

Candidates should be engaged in the opportunity. They should be alert, well-versed on the position, and have a basic understanding of the company. Hey, if some caffeine is in order, so be it! If you're a hiring professional, you know how often the lack of engagement occurs in many of the entry-level positions. Again, people spend an immense amount of time (and sometimes money) to make a great first impression through well-crafted résumés, cover letters, and clothing, only to have it wasted on a totally controllable lack of excitement or energy. That is such a shame. Most managers will tolerate a little *over-the-top* on energy and excitement rather than a *lack of enthusiasm*. Again, just like in a dating relationship, if there is a lack of energy or interest from either party, the relationship will not begin to form.

Hiring Markets

From your perspective as a hiring manager, you may feel that there are many candidates willing, ready and able to accept your position. But maybe not. Let us explain...

There are two types of hiring markets. One is an employer's market and the other is called a candidate's market. As the economy changes, the pendulum swings back and forth from one to the other. In the early 2000s, without question, it was an employer's market. There were very few jobs available and there were numerous candidates available. This allowed employers the ability to interview and hire easily with less competition. In an employer's market, talent is plentiful and abounds in many fields. Because there may be an abundance of candidates to fill limited positions, some organizations take advantage of this scenario in their attitudes and direction.

However, things are different in a candidate's market. When the pendulum swings to a candidate-driven market, the candidates' talents are now in demand, and many times candidates are able to choose from multiple opportunities. This sets a different tone in the job market; employers are no longer in the driver's seat. This can be unfortunate for some prospective employers who do not realize the change has occurred. If they are not as cordial or flexible in their dealings with potential candidates, they will lose a large portion of the available candidate pool during this period.

In a booming economy, such as the one we are experiencing at the time of this publishing, it is much more difficult to find high-quality prospects in some industries because candidates have their choice of job opportunities. In a candidate's market, time is of the essence. Hiring managers need to be aware of how long their hiring process takes and move candidates quickly through each stage so the company does not lose the best candidates to competitors.

Do Unto Others

We know that in your eyes, a candidate must be sincere, passionate, and excited about the opportunity at hand. No question about it, a new hire is a very important decision for you. The quality of this person can be a huge reflection on you and, many times, it will be a direct reflection upon your management and recruiting abilities. With a couple of good hires, you could be on the way to your next promotion. To that point, hiring can be a window into a manager's abilities in front of his or her peers and superiors. Making a wrong choice at this point can be very disruptive and expensive to the organization, along with the cost in lost sales or revenue to the manager's territory, often negatively impacting an entire team.

Hiring quality people is a two-way street. As a manager, you will have many attributes you are looking for in candidates. This is a given. However, in turn, you also need to project the appearance and demeanor necessary to impress the candidate. Yes, as a manager you are an agent of the organization that you work for, and in that role, you also need to be cognizant of how you represent your organization. Arrogance and attitude from a hiring manager may leave the candidate with a negative impression of the company. Did we need to say that? Yes! Sorry, but it does happen! You, as an extraordinary manager, need also be aware that the *great candidate* in front of you may not be totally sold upon the position you are selling. Yes, they may be totally engaged, listening and enthusiastic, but they need your input and confidence. Because you have found the next addition to your team, don't let them down with any negativity. And yes, if you think this is the right person for the job, do your best and sell it! A candidate can be very well prepared after a thorough investigation and research of the company, but they are still looking to you for a feel for the organization and corporate culture. The qualities behind that candidate that have produced the high performance in the past may now be at work evaluating the current environment and your company. So, before that candidate is dismissed due to lack of enthusiasm, maybe you, as a manager, need to do a little selling of your own.

My father once told me a story about a job he interviewed for years ago. When he first interviewed, the manager opened the door for him and was very courteous. In the back of his mind, he thought, "Man, this guy likes me. I might get this job." He was excited about the possibility of working for this person and the company. Then, after the interview, he watched the same manager interact with the human resource department. His demeanor was different with HR. He seemed impatient and demanding. My father said you could tell his attitude was different with the people he worked with every day. My father felt lucky that he had gotten a glimpse of what this manager might be like to work for before he took the position. While your current employees know how you manage, potential employees are also watching how you treat those around you.

Qualities to Evaluate

When you interview a candidate, you are looking for certain qualities that you define as belonging to a *top performer*. Many candidates realize that within those first few minutes, they have only one shot to make a great impression. A great performance could land them back in that seat for the next round of interviews. We're hopeful that upon meeting you, the great candidate will give you a firm handshake, a big smile, and lots of energy and confidence.

Part of the candidate's presentation is listening. We know from experience that listening skills are critical. Did they listen to your question prior to answering?

Additionally, you'll be evaluating them on their appearance, communication skills, attitude, enthusiasm, and technical knowledge. As previously mentioned, we hope the well-prepared candidate will know about your company, as well as being able to demonstrate concrete examples of how they have performed on the job. Also, let's hope they deliver passion in their presentation. Nothing can diminish the impact of significant accomplishments any better than a boring, lackluster delivery. We're not referring to the candidate who can't sit still in the seat during the interview either. Some prospects can come across so energetic during the process that they appear nervous or display a lack confidence or even maturity. However, you have witnessed it before: a dignified level of confidence and enthusiasm can take the well-prepared candidate a very long way, both in the job interview process and this game called life!

Yes, we've talked a little about presentation but it really does merit the attention. If the candidate can't make a strong initial presentation, then why should you be interested? That's a great question. Certain key attributes pertaining to behavior and appearance are important. If a candidate is initially obnoxious or sloppy, that can—and probably should—be an immediate interview failure. Hopefully, through proper initial screening, you can avoid sitting down and wasting precious selection time.

We've found that many candidates have read or at least been coached in creating that all-important initial first impression. They know and understand that the initial presentation must be very positive and elicit a lasting favorable reaction from the interviewer.

You know as a manager that most organizations do not hire upon the first, second, or often, even the third interaction with the candidate. The initial positive impression must survive several regimented and almost grueling interactions in the interview process.

So, what are you looking for when that prospect walks into the room? Well, he or she should have a clean, well-kempt appearance so that you'll form a positive opinion through non-verbal visual cues. How does the candidate do this? One of the most successful ways is to be very well dressed. Wardrobe has been found to be extremely important in the critical first impression. We encourage candidates to simply search the Web for "Professional Business Images."

Again, we know candidates should be excited about the prospective opportunity and display that excitement when they sit down to talk to you. However, not everyone is wired like you. They may see a perfect interview a little differently than you do, and so will some of your co-managers. We are all different; that is what makes teams and organizations dynamic and sometimes downright entertaining. Some people are driven solely by numbers, some are highly social, and some are just flat out *get the job done* types.

How is this relevant to our current discussion? Well, before you make a concrete decision about who's moving forward, consider the needs of your company and various teams. Yes, having great presentation and passion are important qualities for candidates, and we've talked about that at length, but there's much more to the interview process.

We surveyed our panel of hiring managers about the top three qualities they look for in a candidate. Here are a few of their responses:

Top Three Qualities

"1. Sustained Success 2. Trust 3. Humility"

Matt Aultman, District Sales Manager, six years' hiring experience, Pharmaceutical Sales

---

"Depends on the position but in a highly matrixed organization, I look for cross-functional/business big picture experience."

Tracy Barry, Sr. HR Partner, fifteen-plus years' hiring experience, Medical Device, Pharmaceuticals, Financial Services, and Publishing

---

"Resiliency, strategic thinking, collaborative mindset."

David Eberson, Vice President Commercialization, Sales and Service, North America, twenty-five years' hiring experience, Medical Device and Pharmaceuticals

---

"Credibility; coachable; excellent listening skills."

Mike DeMuth, VP Sales, fifteen years' hiring experience in Healthcare Information Technology

---

"1. Good First Impression 2. Strong Education 3. Continuous Work History"

Tom Fowler III, Senior Vice President, State Bank of Southwest Missouri, twenty-three year's hiring experience, Banking

---

"Every position requires different qualities but character, good communication, & work history."

Rita Wright Gurian, Retired Healthcare Executive – Current Non-Profit & Professional Development Coach, thirty-plus years' hiring experience in Healthcare and Non-Profit

---

"Resourcefulness, Drive and Emotional Intelligence"

Ericca Zumaya, Human Resource Generalist, two years hiring experience in Life Sciences/Biotechnology

---

"Integrity, openness to learning and change (flexibility), passion for what they do."

Steve Ford, Senior Manager of New Market Development, twenty-plus years' hiring experience, Pharmaceuticals, Capital Equipment, and Medical Device

---

"Attitude, personality, and experience working with others. Good soft skills and dealing with people are key in any job."

Brent Dunn, Executive Director of Missouri State University Foundation, thirty-five years' hiring experience, Higher Education

---

"Character, Work Ethic, and Intelligence."

Mike Denker, Area Sales Director, twenty-four years' hiring experience, Medical Device and Software

"Passion, work ethic, and adaptability. I like to find the diamond in the rough who can produce high volumes of work, who has growth potential and is looking to make an impact. Change is inevitable, so being fluid and adaptable is a must for growth."

Seda Onek, Human Resources Manager, ten-plus years' experience, Medical Device

"Enthusiasm/excitement, Detail-oriented, maintain good eye contact."

Reggie Steward, Regional Sales Director, two years' hiring experience, Medical Sales

"Coachability, Prior Success, and Passion."

Todd Derickson, Director of Sales, twenty-plus year's hiring experience, Medical Device

"Integrity/Honesty, Self-Awareness, and Communication/Critical Thinking skills."

Greg Burris, President & CEO, thirty years' hiring experience, United Way of the Ozarks, Nonprofit Impact Previous experience in higher education at Missouri State University, and in city government as City Manager for the City of Springfield, Missouri

"Loyalty, passion, past performance"

Marc Waldman, VP Business Development, twenty years' hiring experience, Medical Device

Chapter Seven

Kindle the Fire

By asking questions regarding their functionality, integrity, results, and evaluating their level of enthusiasm, you should have an idea of which candidates you are interested in moving forward following your first interview. Each of these candidates should have the pillars identified in the job description you created. The question at this point changes to "How do I keep these candidates interested?" This is the stage of the interview process we call "kindling the fire."

As we said in the previous chapter, common courtesy dictates that organizations need to positively interact with candidates on all levels. Managers need to be prompt on telephone interviews, be keenly aware of other people's time, particularly in relation to traveling to interviews, and be wary of making unrealistic expectations during the selection process. They need to level the playing field, not only to abide by EEOC guidelines but because it's the right thing to do.

Discussing both sides of the equation between the employer and potential employee gets right back to where we started. Both parties need to "spark" their relationship early; this begins with the first interview or interaction. Though a business relationship is being established, the final thoughts and considerations will be made by a person. This decision-maker is no different than the countless others we've interacted with in the business world over the years. They have their own views and unique perspectives, and a connection with those perspectives can help seal the deal. The candidate with drive and initiative during and throughout the interview process will be supported by being selected. The thought that *this person can do the job* needs to be constant throughout the process. Displaying the energy and ability to learn the key activities places an ideal candidate in the driver's seat above those simply with the credentials alone. Maybe interviewers think that John *could* run a marathon, but would he? Whereas, they're convinced that Steve *will* run the marathon and accomplish a lot along the way.

Relationships sell the candidate. The above scenario between the candidates' abilities points to their ability to "sell" during the interview process. This selling ability is based primarily upon the beliefs developed during the establishment of the early relationship in the selection process. The candidates who win the position display and maintain a high level of energy, passion, excitement, and conviction from start to finish.

Really, we practice relationship building in all facets of our daily lives. Think back on how you may have developed relationships within your own life. Much work and effort go into the things that we desire. As an example, I met my husband-to-be (Randy) late one night at a restaurant. I had just finished working the evening shift at the local hospital as an RN in an oncology wing. I was there with my nurse friend, Diane, and Randy was there with his buddy, Dennis. We were both customers, and the waitresses just happened to seat us at tables across from one another. Because we were seated in such close proximity, Randy began a conversation with me by introducing himself.

From the first moments we met, he showed he was interested by asking where I worked and who I might know. With this question, we were able to discover we knew several of the same people. As the conversation continued, we discovered other similarities. This is one of the reasons I felt attracted to him. He was not afraid to communicate; he showed respect, and he showed an interest in me. Later, because my phone number was unlisted, he had to do some research to secure it. After he received my number from one of my friends, he called me for a lunch date, and the rest is history.

Interviewing is no different. In fact, it is much more difficult than a dating relationship because of time constraints. During an interview, both the candidate and the employer only have a few minutes to make a lasting impression on each other. The thirty to sixty minutes spent during an interview not only determine if the candidate *gets* the job, but it also determines if the candidate *wants* the job. Keep in mind that while it is not always an employers' job market as we discussed previously, candidates in most situations still have a healthy *choice* in which company they choose, given that they are qualified and talented.

Just like a dating relationship, we contend that there are three basic principles that can be brought into the employer-employee relationship to help make it work. These are:

Interest in the other party

Respect
On-going communication.

Just like putting logs on a fire to kindle the flames, these principles will ignite your relationship. One of the most important decisions we make in life is choosing the right person to be our partner. It could also be said that some of the most important decisions we make as managers are choosing the right employees.

To get the right employees interested in your company, you might need to think of the interview process a little differently. Candidates today are not just looking for their next job—they want to work for companies that share a similar world view so that they can make a difference. Start by asking yourself these questions: Why would this candidate want to work for my organization? What will working for this company do to help this individual, and how will it help their career growth?

Many interviewers make up their mind about a candidate based on the first five minutes of their initial meeting. In turn, great candidates can make up their mind about a company within the first few minutes of the interview too. That is the biggest reason to understand the principles of *HIRE with FIRE*.

> **"During the next twenty-plus years, the competition for talent is going to be fierce. Organizations who excel at recruiting and retaining talent are going to have a massive competitive advantage."**
>
> *Greg Burris, President & CEO, United Way of the Ozarks, thirty years' hiring experience, Non-profit, Higher Education, City Government- former City Manager for the City of Springfield, Missouri*

To Ghost or Not to Ghost

Time is critical during the interview process. If you have completed your first interview, then keep it moving. We've seen companies wait weeks before doing a second interview and then lose most, sometimes all, of the candidates they were interested in moving forward. If you are not able to do the second interview within seven days, then reach out to let the candidate know why. In a recent study by Indeed, 27% of candidates in 18-34 year-old age group decided not to interview further with a company because of a lengthy application period, while only 18% of the 45-to 65-year-old cohorts did the same. This may suggest that younger candidates may have different expectations about the length of the recruitment process whereas older generations have a more realistic understanding.[6]

Top talent is in demand. Delays in your process may cause you to lose the candidates and have to start all over again. Just like a dating

---

[6] Indeed 2019. *The Ghosting Guide: An Inside Look at Why Job Seekers Disappear.* August 26. Accessed August 27,2019
http://blog.indeed.com/2019/08/26/ghosting-guide/.

relationship, if a person doesn't contact you after you meet with them and ask to meet again, you assume they are not interested.

As professionals, we know that not every interaction with a candidate works out. Maybe you have met with a candidate and feel they do not have the skills necessary to perform the job, or maybe you feel that they just wouldn't fit into your organization or team. Whatever the reason, there just wasn't a spark, and you are ready to end the relationship. Again, whether you want to admit it or not, it is a relationship. You met with someone, discussed an opportunity and potentially got their hopes up. So, where do you go from here? How do you let the person know they are not going to be moving forward?

The truth is, it isn't always easy, but it is necessary. If you were dating someone and then didn't want to see them again, wouldn't you let them know? Oftentimes, people just try to fade away from the relationship, a term referred to today as "ghosting." But this lack of response actually portrays a lack of respect for the individual. The dictionary defines ghosting as "the act or practice of abruptly cutting off all contact with someone (such as a former romantic partner) by no longer accepting or responding to phone calls, instant messages, etc."[7] In fact, in the same Indeed survey of over 4,000 job seekers and nearly 900 employers across multiple industries, 18% of job seekers say they have been ghosted by an employer at some point during the hiring process.[8]

You have probably heard the term *ghosting* many times but have not thought about the impacts of it on your company. The sad fact is that potential candidates will remember how they were treated during the interview process, and this will impact your reputation, your company's reputation, and your ability to hire top talent in the future. Additionally, several internet websites offer company reviews as a venue to record their experiences for all to see.

> **"After face to face interviews, I do call the candidates that did not get the job offer. I usually tell them why we hired the successful candidate."**
>
> *Brent Dunn, Vice-President, Office of University Advancement, Executive Director of Missouri State University Foundation, thirty-five years' hiring experience, Higher Education*

> **"We notify them via phone and if they ask for feedback we provide it."**
>
> *Mike DeMuth, VP Sales, fifteen years' hiring experience in Healthcare Information Technology*

Turning On the Charm

If the first interview went well, you might want to start turning on the charm. As we have discussed, your relationship with this person has

---

[7] Merriam Webster, Accessed July 8, 2019 through https://www.merriam-webster.com/dictionary/ghosting

[8] Indeed 2019. *The Ghosting Guide: An Inside Look at Why Job Seekers Disappear.* August 26. Accessed August 27, 2019 http://blog.indeed.com/2019/08/26/ghosting-guide/ .

now begun. Trust needs to be established early. You started evaluating them based upon multiple factors. One of these factors may be whether the potential candidate sends you a thank you note after their interview with you. Many managers feel this is critical, and it is customary in the business world for the candidate to send a thank you or follow-up note. But wait a minute—do you realize that most managers never respond to the candidate's thank you note? By responding to your potential candidate, you show them your interest level and provide critical communication during a time when your relationship is in the development stage. If it were an actual note from a friend, wouldn't you respond?

Recently, we had a hiring manager respond to a thank you note from a candidate. It was a simple acknowledgment: "Thank you for your time and effort invested in this opportunity." Wow! That was all it took for the candidate to want to work for this manager. He felt valued and respected. You might wonder if this gets a candidate's hopes up. After all, you're not sure you are going to offer them the position, right? Maybe so, but it is good old-fashion courtesy to thank someone for their time and effort. In this email, the manager was not telling the candidate if he was getting the position—he was just acknowledging the candidate's thank you note and building a potential future relationship.

I know that this may sound counterintuitive because it is not how the process is usually done. Traditionally, candidates are supposed to send their interviewers a thank you note, not the other way around. In the past that might have been the case; however, consider the difference it would make in the process if you did something unexpected by responding to the candidate. It doesn't have to be a complicated thank you note, and it doesn't need to lead them on by suggesting they'll get the job. It could be just a few words to let them know what the next step will be so they do not feel ghosted. If you are still evaluating other candidates, let them know. They will appreciate your honesty and will remain interested because you showed an interest in them.

This type of activity is what we call "kindling the fire" with the potential new hire. When you "kindle the fire," you create a passion that will last long after the interview process ends. You create a relationship with that person. Remember, we all want to work for a company that we can believe in and have a manager who believes in us. By being respectful of the candidate's time, you will get their buy-in on the job, your company, and you as a manager. Who knows, you may not end up hiring that person to work for you, but chances are you may run into them again in the future in some other professional situation. It's hard to fix a burned bridge.

We used the example of the thank you note because we want you to think differently about the interview process. If you want to attract the best individuals to your organization, you will do so with being courteous of their time. Today's generation of workers—including millennials, Gen Xers, and younger generations—want to feel wanted and respected. They want to make a difference and provide value to an organization and to the world. This is often more important to them than status, titles, or money.

That being the case, how do you make a good impression on a potential candidate? You may draw attention to the way you as an employer are unique from other contenders. For example, my daughter dated a guy who asked her out again at the end of the first date instead of waiting to call. By doing this, he demonstrated that he was already thinking of when they could be together again. He was confirming his interest in her. Think about this in the context of interviewing. If you are interested in the candidate sitting in front of you, why not ask them if they would be available for a second interview? This creates interest for both parties and will more than likely make the candidate excited to move on in the process. Remember, your relationship has already begun with this person, so it is important to continue the relationship in a positive way.

There is really no excuse for not treating others with respect and dignity, especially during the recruiting and hiring process. Probably the biggest complaint we hear as recruiters is that some companies do not provide feedback about a person's candidacy. Most candidates welcome this feedback, even to hear that they are no longer being considered for the job. At this point, they can move on to other opportunities. Again, keep in mind this is a relationship. Wouldn't it be great if your company became an industry benchmark for its hiring practices? How do candidates view your management team and your organizational culture? Would changing your interviewing techniques improve your employer brand?

♠ CHAPTER EIGHT

The Second "Date"

For the second "date" to occur, you must have done something right on the first "date." Otherwise, the person would not have agreed to meet with you again, right? Well, not necessarily. You may have just piqued their curiosity. This isn't a bad thing.

Many hiring managers assume that candidates interview because they need another job when often candidates interview simply out of curiosity. Maybe their interest was piqued by an advertisement or a call from a recruiter, or maybe they are not content in their current job. Sometimes people interview just because they want to know that they are still employable and desired by other companies. Again, this is like dating. People date for various reasons, not always to find true love. Sometimes, people date because they want to feel wanted by someone or even just for entertainment. In other words, don't assume that a candidate is interested in your opportunity. They may be just "playing the field."

Common feedback we receive from candidates is that the interview questions seemed to lack direct relevance. Sometimes an interview question that is off-topic may be asked just to allow the interview to check a candidate's mental acuity. Top talent deserves well-thought-out questions that are directly related to the position. Avoiding the "What is the meaning of life?" type questions will earn you credibility both in the interview process and as a future employer.

Just as you may lose interest in a candidate due to a barrage of ancillary or unnecessary information, your best candidate may lose interest due to indirect, seemingly irrelevant questions. If there seems to be a lack of focus or organization in the interview, specifically in the questioning, the candidate may get the impression that the organization itself lacks focus or a certain degree of professionalism. Remember, you've carefully screened the individuals that you want to interview and they deserve your best, just like you expect the best from them. We coach candidates daily in preparation for tough, professional interviews. Through the candidates' careful analysis of your company and the job itself, they have spent a considerable amount of time in preparation, so give them your best.

Some key areas that interviewers might cover before meeting their candidate pool a second time could be an in-depth analysis of the job description. It's essential to review the key competencies and skill sets that individuals need to possess and compare them to those that may have some future benefit to the organization. Look closely at the position. What challenges exist that need to be addressed, and how can specific candidates make a difference? Outside of the minimum criteria, what individual traits are you looking for? Do you need someone who is more gregarious and amiable in nature or more analytical?

After a review of the necessary competencies and skill sets, understand that the second interview is a great time to start bragging about your company. If you have a great training program, 401(k) retirement plan, or opportunities for advancement, let the candidate know now. Discuss the salary, commissions, bonuses, and any other benefits that interest the candidate. Candidates are taught that it is not acceptable for them to bring up these questions too early. However, this information can make or break their interest in your organization so don't wait until the offer stage to discuss it. Make sure you know exactly what they are looking for in their next career move. There should be no surprises.

Keep in mind that the second interview is an extremely vital time in the interview process. It's not a time to assume anything about the person or their interest in the position. Typically, after a candidate has already met with you twice, they are interested in the position, and they think you are very serious about them as a candidate. However, just like when dating, it's hard to always know when the other party is sincere and is still interested in moving the relationship forward. Your favorite candidate could also be interviewing with a couple of other companies and be further along in their process, so this is no time to slow down.

At this juncture, you hopefully have some insight into why the candidate is interested in your open position and why they want to make a job change. If you don't know by now, ask them. There are many reasons people change jobs. Sometimes it is money, but oftentimes it is something about their current duties, company policies, or manager's management style.

By asking your potential candidate why they are considering a job change, you can learn more about what motivates them. For instance, in a sales role, a candidate might respond better to a compensation plan that is more commissioned-based than salary-driven. This information is valuable when it's time to offer them the position. If they can see your management style is different than their previous employer and that your company supports their career objectives, they will want to join your team.

Avoid Surface Interviewing

Throughout the interview process, you will be in what we call the discovery mode. Just like a lawyer uses discovery to obtain evidence about the case, you are seeking to discover more about this potential employee. To do this, you will need to avoid surface interviewing.

What do we mean? *Surface interviewing* means you don't fully "dive in" with questioning this individual. You meet your candidate; they seem nice, and you never get around to fully understanding what makes them tick, their career goals, background, and accomplishments. As recruiters, we see this all the time when managers are not properly trained, or they don't prepare for interviews ahead of time.

The first interview allows you to establish a bond with a potential employee early, like discussing your favorite sports team or industry friends, but after that initial interview, you will need to dive in. Go deeper in questioning this individual. I am not talking about asking personal questions that would be considered discriminatory like age or familial status. You should ask questions that allow you to see how this potential employee would handle a situation or how they would fit into your organization. Learn more about their career goals. Just like a lawyer preparing for a big case, your goal is to discover all you can about the other party *before* you hire them, not afterward. You can do this by asking well-thought-out questions that go beyond the surface.

We asked our panel of hiring managers to share their favorite interview question. On the following pages, you will find a few of their responses. These are examples of deeper questions that will help you get to know your candidate better.

Favorite Interview Questions from Our Panel of Hiring Managers

"'What have your previous leaders told you that you need to work on?' Tests their integrity, self-awareness, strategic thinking and many other areas. If they give a benign response that tells me a lot and if they package something in a clever way—it tells me a lot also—but in a good way."

David Eberson, Vice President Commercialization, Sales and Service, North America, twenty-five years' hiring experience, Medical Device and Pharmaceuticals

"'Who was the greatest influence in your life, and what good things will you do this week as a result of that influence?'"

Mike Denker, Area Sales Director, twenty-four years' hiring experience, Medical Device and Software

"I always ask to talk about a failure they had and what they learned from it. I like to see how honest they are and not just 'spin' a failure. I want to know what they consider their weakness."

Brent Dunn, Executive Director of Missouri State University Foundation, thirty-five years' hiring experience, Higher Education

---

"It is a very simple question with many ramifications. I always ask 'Where do you want your career to go from this point?' I want to get into the psychology of what their ambition is and I would spend most of the interview trying to get that candidate comfortable enough to be very truthful with me in regards to that question. It also helps that my interview style is very laid back, more of a conversationalist style. It allows them to feel free to open up more than your traditional 'canned' questions from an inexperienced hiring manager."

Todd Derickson, Director of Sales, twenty-plus year's hiring experience, Medical Device

---

"What have you heard about our institution?' It is impressive to have an applicant that has researched our company prior to interview."

Tom Fowler III, Senior Vice President, State Bank of Southwest Missouri, twenty-three year's hiring experience, Banking

---

"What interests you about this job and why would you be a good fit?"

Rita Wright Gurian, Retired Healthcare Executive—Current Non-Profit & Professional Development Coach, thirty-plus years' hiring experience in Healthcare and Non-Profit

"What are the three personal attributes you feel have helped you be successful so far in your career?"

Steve Ford, Senior Manager of New Market Development, twenty-plus years' hiring experience, Pharmaceuticals, Capital Equipment, and Medical Device

"I love asking about what motivates the candidate. It is such a simple question but gives you so much insight into who they are. I hire for passion above anything else, and knowing what drives them helps me see their potential. That usually ties into where they see themselves in the long term, and what they are passionate about."

Seda Onek, Human Resources Manager, ten-plus years' experience, Medical Device

"'What did you do to prepare for this interview?' I like to see more than just, 'I looked at the company's website.'"

Reggie Steward, Regional Sales Director, two years' hiring experience, Medical Sales

"What do you want to be when you grow up?"

Marc Waldman, VP Business Development, twenty years' hiring experience, Medical Device

"'What is your greatest professional accomplishment? Did you accomplish anything else similar to it afterwards?' I like this question because all candidates have their favorite 'impressive' story about what they have done in the past, though the follow-up question shows whether or not that accomplishment was a one-time occurrence or if they are the type of person who continually accomplishes large wins."

Ericca Zumaya, Human Resource Generalist, two years' hiring experience in Life Sciences/Biotechnology

Meeting Your Family

After your second interview with the candidate, what's the next step? How do you continue to make sure you are hiring the best person for the job? Well, if it were a dating situation, you might want them to meet some of your friends or maybe even members of your family. If we continue thinking of interviews as the start of a great relationship, you would be correct. Why not have them meet your friends and family? In this case, your friends and family are the other leaders within the company or potential coworkers. Let's get their input. This is an important interviewing validation phase. You are involving other corporate players to take a look at the candidate too. This will allow additional input on the hiring decision.

> **"...We like to have stakeholders that will work with the candidate as well as peers have an opportunity to meet the candidate as well."**
>
> *Tracy Barry, Sr. HR Partner, fifteen-plus years' hiring experience, Medical Device, Pharmaceuticals, Financial Services, and Publishing*

During this process, it is important to make sure that each team member understands that they should closely follow EEOC guidelines and ask questions that are relevant and not discriminatory. Issues may be created when candidates are screened by team members who are not properly trained in EEOC standards. I once was interviewed by a physician for a management position at a clinic. The physician asked me how old I was and if I was going to have any children. While a great physician, the person was not aware that their questions were discriminatory in nature.

But before you set up these meetings with other staff, switch gears and think of yourself at your next team meeting. Let's take a look at the social element of your next hire. Will this person fit in with the existing team? Consider the needs of your company and the personality style of an individual that will help build your business. Building business is of key importance but so is adding an individual who will help add to the synergy and stability of the team.

The point is this: sometimes a great candidate may be eliminated simply because of a manager's personal preference, not because they lack real qualifications to do the job. They can do the job well, yet their delivery of their abilities is lacking. They may be very passionate about the position in their own ways, but not very expressive. However, these individuals can deliver clinical or technical data in a very credible manner. Because they approach business in a different fashion does not make them wrong or a bad candidate. In fact, the opposite may be true. Your team can benefit from their diversity. Truly, a candidate is not defined by how he or she may appear in his or her initial presentation. They may have the background, contacts, successes, and education that you feel you need, but may still be missing something in your eyes. Well, as you are aware, there are many distinct personality types, and although you may migrate to an expressive driver-type personality, an analytical driver can produce the same stellar results in a very different way. [9]

The Ability to Coach and the "Driver" Personality

Virtually all managers want to hire assertive, high-energy performers when they look at new additions to their teams. And why wouldn't they? Typically, these folks are the ones who can make the biggest impact on the bottom line, which of course is to produce great numbers that can propel forward their team's rankings and potentially enhance the manager's career. However, as we look toward locating talented employees, we also need to consider the amiable side of a candidate's personality. These are the tendencies that will help the individual thrive in a team environment and build upon the talents of others. Amiable drivers function well on a team and many times aspire for and are successful in management roles.

These individuals are hard workers, major influencers, and are experts in promoting the agenda at hand. Yes, maybe the predominant personality of your next hire should be a driver, but don't overlook what makes an employee endearing both in personality and tenure. Strong relationship skills, sincere desire and the ability to win creates a winning team for all! True drivers with amiable tendencies are not easy to find. You'll need to have examples of personality types to reference during the interview process just like you do with the performance section of your interview. Sure, your battery of questions probably has personality questions, but many times they are overshadowed by the desire to look at performance only. Astute managers should look at their recruits in totality. Assessing the whole package prior to hiring can save you grief in

---

[9] Merrill, David, Personal Styles and Effective Performance, CRC Press, Merrill-Reid

dealing with interpersonal issues and help you continue to build your dynamic team.

Therefore, it is so important to have a team approach in the interviewing process. For instance, if your team consists of ten individuals, you may want to select one or two of these folks to also interview a potential candidate. This will give your team members a chance to provide feedback on the candidate, and the candidate can receive a unique, fresh insight into the applied-for position. Additionally, this will give the candidate an easy way to fit into the company's culture if offered the position.

Allowing a potential candidate to interact with other leaders and team members will show confidence in your company's culture. Some of our clients allow a day working alongside another employee or a ride-along—in the case of sales—or an internship in which the potential candidate see firsthand how the job is done. This allows for open communication and assists in relationship building.

We once had a candidate do a ride-along with a current employee (a field sales representative) and after their interaction, the current employee complained to the manager about the candidate's behavior during the ride-along. It was eye-opening. The employee described how the candidate changed the radio station in their car to another station several times without asking first. This came across as disrespectful to the employee hosting the ride-along. In this situation, the candidate showed no signs of disrespect during the two face-to-face interviews with the manager, but this event provided insight on how the candidate might eventually interact with coworkers and, potentially, customers.

By allowing some of your current employees to talk to potential employees, your company displays an open-door policy where communication is promoted within the organization. Most potential employees will appreciate the information.

Will They Fit In? Understanding Your Organizational Culture

Understanding your organizational culture is important in hiring the right individuals. If a candidate has worked for a small start-up company, will they fit in at a Fortune 500 company and vice versa? How flexible are they, and how do you feel they would adapt with such a change?

Start by defining the culture of your organization. What type of communication does your organization utilize? Hopefully, a little bit of both upward and downward communication. According to Mathis and Jackson, "Downward communication flows from top management to the rest of the organization, informing employees about what is and will be happening in the organization, and what the expectations and goals of top management are. Upward communication enables managers to learn about the ideas, concerns, and information needs of employees."[10] In other words, upward communication allows employees to be more involved. We have discovered over the past few decades, as newer generations entered the workforce, communication has drastically changed. With several generations in the workforce, communication has never been more vital. Today, our workforce is comprised of:

- Traditionalists—born before 1946.
- Baby Boomers—born between 1946 and 1964.
- Generation X—born between 1965 and 1976.
- Generation Y, or millennials—born between 1977 and 1997.*
- Generation Z—born after 1997.[11]

Note: *Other sources say that millennials can be born between 1981 and 1996.[12]

Each generation communicates differently, so by using both upward and downward communication within your organization, the groups will remain connected and you may experience less friction. Although many means of communication are considered formal, electronic communication is often seen as easiest and more widespread. How does your organization share vital information to your employees and

[10] Mathis, Robert L., and Jackson, John H. Human Resource Management (2008), Twelfth Edition. South-Western Cengage Learning, Mason, OH. Pg.510

[11] Lin Grensing-Pophal (2018) How to Handle 5 Generations in the Workplace, Diversity Insight, Accessed by July 8, 2019 through https://hrdailyadvisor.blr.com/2018/02/26/handle-5-generations-workplace/

[12] Dimock, Michael. 2019. *Defining generations: Where Millennials end and Generation Z begins.* January 17. Accessed August 24, 2019. https://www.pewresearch.org/fact-tank/2019/01/17/where-millennials-end-and-generation-z-begins/.

does that form of communication work well? Once you define your organizational culture, you may want to create an interview question that will help you gain insight into the individual and how they would transition to your culture. This type of question may be in regard to how they handle change and to what degree they have the flexibility to change.

Check them out

You have made your selection and decided on one or two people to move forward to the final interview process. Now it is time to check them out. In today's world, fraud is prevalent, so background checks are extremely important! Always do a background check! Someone may not be who they say they are.

Several years ago, I was catfished. If you don't know that word, it means that someone intentionally tries to swindle you, often by pretending to be someone else. If you can believe it, my dog, Patches, a two-year-old dachshund & terrier mix, and rescue dog actually catfished me. Bet you didn't think a dog could do such a thing! Let me explain further.

The rescue shelter had listed Patches as a poodle/terrier mix on its website. I just happened to be looking for a dog but wanted to get a poodle due to pet allergies. When I saw his profile online, I was excited to go visit the poodle named Patches.

Randy, my daughter, and I went to the rescue shelter to see Patches. When we arrived, we couldn't find him. There were no poodles, and no dogs named Patches. We decided he must have been adopted and that we would try to find a poodle another time. I thought it must not have been meant to be. But just before we left, our daughter noticed a dog sitting quietly in the corner. His name tag was flipped up but he had black spots all over his body. When she flipped the name tag down, low and behold, there was Patches from the Internet.

Well, Patches was definitely not a poodle, so I was very reluctant to adopt him. With his long hair, I was worried about my allergy issues. After all, this is not the dog I had in mind. However, I quickly gave in as Randy and our daughter fell in love with his gentle spirit. We decided this was the dog we wanted.

Now the story does have a happy ending! It's been over seven years since that day, and Patches is a valuable member of our family. I think Patches can be a little bit of a con artist at times, especially since his online profile was done like a professional *catfish*: giving potentially false breed identity to get adopted. All kidding aside, I am glad he is a member of our family, and I know his profile was not listed that way intentionally. Things have a way of working out. As for my pet allergies, I guess that is what allergy medicine is for!

I used that story as an example. Unfortunately, people may not always be honest about the reason they left their last position or what accomplishments they achieved, so do your due diligence prior to hiring. Once you have thoroughly vetted someone, you will feel more comfortable with them, and your relationship will be stronger.

Let me tell you a quick story about my mother. She was a switchboard operator in the 1950s in Germany after the war. Every day, she would show her identification to the military police as she entered the base to go to her job. My father, her future husband, was one of the military police who would check her pass.

As they began to know each other, she decided she really liked him. She thought that he might be a few years younger than she was and didn't want this to become an issue, so she put an inkblot over the birth year on her identification card. She was five years older than he was. This seemed to work out fine for her since she looked young for her age. It only became an issue when she later had to disclose her real age to the Justice of the Peace on their wedding day. The story also ends well, obviously. They were married over fifty years and had one lovely daughter (me).

My mom was full of determination and integrity, so this story makes me laugh. It is a great example of how relationships can develop, despite obstacles, when people have passion. Also, not everything or everybody or every situation is always as it seems. People may not literally put inkblots on their résumé, but they may leave off information that might be important. Background checks offer valuable insight into a person's past, so don't leave out this important step. Before you decide to continue a relationship with this person by allowing them to become a part of your organization, check them out. Some inkblots may not be a problem, but others might be.

By now, you have completed several rounds of interviews with this candidate. You have completed a background check and you feel you have the person that is a great fit for your team. Congratulations, you are moving things in the right direction. You have started the fire— now let's keep it burning.

♦ CHAPTER NINE

The Proposal

You have found the perfect match. Good for you! Now it is time to offer them the position. Where do you start? A well-written offer letter will save you a lot of time and secure the candidate's interest in the position. Looking back at the dating relationship analogy, when giving an offer to a candidate, make sure you start with an engagement ring, not a promise ring. In other words, be fully onboard with your offer and don't be cut-rate. Recently, one of our clients made an offer to a candidate. The candidate was excited about the position; however, they rejected the offer because it was only

$2,000 more in salary than they were making in their last posi_____. This is what we would call the non-committal promise ring instead of the engagement ring. Ask any girl—a promise ring is nice, but the real goal is the engagement ring! The candidate needs to know that you are invested!

The workforce is full of talent. The challenge resides in attempting to secure the very best in the industry and entice them to join your team. Many top-notch professionals may feel secure and fairly happy with their current employment. That's a problem for you as a manager when you're trying to entice these folks to transition and join your team.

You may want to work with your HR partners to develop an employer value proposition statement (EVP) for your company. This statement defines your organizational culture and gives the candidate reasons to be interested in working for your company. It can include financial rewards, your environment, fun things your company does, the work you do, and how it impacts the world. Statistics show that 70 % of a company's brand is determined by "people experience."[13] By creating a positive image in the candidate's mind with a comprehensive EVP statement you may attract more talent, increase retention, and lift morale.

How do you proceed with your plan to attract new talent? Well, just like the government entices new businesses by lowering property taxes or sales taxes, you attract talented people to your company by offering benefits.

---

[13] Barac, Dino, (2016) Twelve Stats Every HR Professional Needs to Know About Employer Branding, Accessed July 10, 2019 through
https://www.linkedin.com/pulse/employer-branding-statistics-infographic-dino-bara

Components of the Employment Offer

Let's first look at what might already be offered in your company to bring in the best talent:

Sign-on Bonus

This type of new hire bonus is usually reserved to recruit candidates with critical skill sets and where there is a documented shortage of individuals in the marketplace. This may be legitimized due to difficulty in recruiting and retention issues. The amount is generally no more than twenty percent of the first year's salary.

Increased Base Salary

Many times we find candidates are unwilling to move for less than a ten percent increase in salary. If the increase is not significant enough, it could potentially be considered a lateral move, unless other incidentals are added. Often 25 to 40 percent may be in order, especially if there are significant differences in housing costs or the overall cost of living in an area. Additionally, many candidates switch companies to assume a higher position with more associated responsibilities. If it is more of an apple-to-apple comparison, a range of 12 to 20 percent may be needed to facilitate the move.

Commission/Bonus Structure

Although many times it's not a concrete number, we find that many candidates are willing to switch employers based upon potential increases in gross income. For instance, a candidate at company A is making $125,000 base in their current job. Company B approaches the candidate and offers to match their base salary and benefits package but offers them quarterly bonuses at plan plus a commission structure. Company A has offered a meager bonus structure that provides $20,000 over the year at plan. Thus, total compensation resides at $145,000. Knowing their capacity and the business at hand, the candidate feels comfortable taking the new position with the knowledge that they will receive, in addition to their base salary, a commission of 7 percent of gross sales in the $1 million territory. The total compensation for the new gig would be $195,000, effectively increasing their compensation by $50,000 per year over their old job.

Vacation Time

Many times adding additional vacation time may facilitate a move if the employee is looking for a better work-life balance.

Tuition Reimbursement

Tuition reimbursement is included in many benefit packages. However, its use varies considerably. Some employees find that it's difficult to give 100 percent at work and have time for additional schooling. The collateral concern is that the employee fears their manager feels this way as well! The company must embrace tuition reimbursement at all levels for it to be a legitimate perk, and many simply don't! Sometimes companies that offer tuition reimbursement do so with the premise that the employee must commit to remaining with the company for a specified time after they get their degree.

Other Benefit Packages

Health benefit packages can vary greatly as well. Sometimes these benefits are undervalued by prospective employees, simply because they are not sold to the potential employee as a significant benefit to their employment with the company. Some health insurance programs may pay 50 percent of premiums, while others pay nearly all of these premium costs. Some companies will cover new employees immediately, while others require a 90- to 180-day waiting period. Additionally, ancillary coverage such as dental, vision, life, and disability coverage may or may not be a part of a company's package. Health care benefits may also be offered to retirees, which is a considerable bonus in today's times. An informed candidate will consider the differences between their current coverage and the offered coverage with the prospect organization.

In addition, some companies offer corporate wellness programs, including physical fitness, mental health care, financial programs, assistance with student loan debt, and caring for aging parents. As we mentioned, improved work-life balance can also be a benefit as more employees are tasked with taking care of their aging parents in addition to their own family. According to Gallup, "53% of employees say a role that allows them to have greater work-life balance and better personal well-being is 'very important' to them."[14]

> **"We currently offer a dog and infant friendly headquarters. I've seen company's provide onsite daycare and unlimited PTO."**
>
> *Ericca Zumaya, Human Excellence Generalist, two years' hiring experience in Life Sciences/Biotechnology*

Retirement

Although overlooked by many, a retirement package can be important. Many companies are moving away from a retirement package in favor of contribution to a company-sponsored savings program, such as a 401(k) plan. Again, companies may contribute or match a significant portion of savings, providing an added benefit to the employee. Where available, retirement packages can be an addition to the company-sponsored savings plan, which can provide a significantly increased nest egg for future retirement years.

Profit-Sharing and Stock Options

Profit-sharing generally includes a percentage of company profits placed aside to divide up between qualified employees. All employees can be included or just a portion, such as executives. Additionally, stock options are sometimes offered to employees to provide them a potential future gain if the company grows.

---

[14] Gallup, State of the American Workplace (2017) p.26 Accessed July 11, 2019 through https://www.gallup.com/workplace/238085/state-american-workplace-report-2017.aspx

Changes in Title

Recently, I worked with a candidate who was looking for a promotion that was more important to them than a specific monetary amount. My client was able to change the title of a position to encompass the candidate's career goals. Sometimes, it is the little things that matter most.

As we know, there is a myriad of corporate benefits that include the aforementioned and many, many more not referenced or even in existence yet! As a representative of your organization, it's important to establish those benefits of true importance. What do employees really expect, and what type of benefits will help draw talent to your organization? Determine what benefits are nice to have versus those that will shine within your industry.

Leadership Training

Leadership training is another area to consider as a benefit. Job enlargement and enrichment programs will help you to develop your staff. Job enlargement is generally an expansion of current job responsibilities, potentially making the position more challenging. The tasks are generally more lateral in nature and thereby on the same organizational level. Job enrichment, like the name implies, is used to provide greater satisfaction within the role. It may involve giving additional roles and responsibilities to an individual that are normally completed by a more senior-level individual.

"We also have accelerated Leadership Programs based on the level of the associate so we have an early career Emerging Leader Program, a Mid-Level Manager and a GM Accelerator Program."

Tracy Barry, Sr. HR Partner, fifteen-plus years' hiring experience, Medical Device, Pharmaceuticals, Financial Services and Publishing

In either case, these motivational techniques are used to foster a better employee experience and enhance their overall satisfaction. By doing so, an organization hopes to increase their employee retention.

A strong retention may indicate to a potential new hire that the company is a stable place to work. In today's world, stability is a sought-after benefit, especially to those who have been laid off previously.

As employees continue to grow as individuals, your hope is that they will continue to grow in their job as well. In turn, these stellar employees will also provide your company with future leadership during times of organizational growth. By developing leadership qualities in your employees, you will promote your staff to think outside of the box, which will help them in all of their duties.

The Offer Letter

All of the previous areas discussed should be considered and included, if applicable, when making an official offer to a candidate. If the candidate does not see all the information in a written offer, they may not accept the position. Obviously, if there is not an acceptance, then somewhere the process has failed. It could be a breakdown in communication about the terms of the offer or a lack of buy-in earlier in the interview process. Ultimately, if this happens you have wasted your time and the candidate's time.

Take a look at the template offer letter your company is using. Does it showcase your company and organization's culture? Would you be excited to receive it? As recruiters, we have seen offer letters that were just that—a letter offering the job. It had the usual information, salary, and start date. But what if we think about the offer letter in the sense that it is a proposal? Would you want someone to propose to you with just the basic information, or would you want a gesture that was more expressive and interesting? Maybe you would want to have something you could tell your grandchildren about in years to come?

Remember when we discussed giving someone a promise ring instead of the engagement ring? Well, an offer letter that is well-written is like an engagement ring—it shows your interest in the person. This is the time to get them excited about working for your company. It is the engagement ring and the "I Do" all wrapped up into one. If the person accepts your offer, then the relationship is official.

Here are some ideas to consider in your future offer letters:

- Use a cover sheet with your logo, an inviting photo of your company, perhaps inside the lobby, and company mission statement.
- Use a header, such as, "Join ABC Company and help us change XXX."
- Include a letter from the CEO or top leader in your organization discussing your organization's mission, culture, and why you offer employee benefits.
- Include leadership's contact information (CEO, CFO, HR and hiring manager).
- Include the basics: title of position, salary, start date, commission plans, benefits, at-will employment relationships, and any other contingencies, such as background checks and drug screens.
- Include an acceptance time frame relative to dates.

These are just a few ways to start your relationship off right. Next, we will discuss what happens after the proposal is accepted.

♠ CHAPTER TEN

The Engagement

Yahoo! It's time to celebrate. You offered your proposal and the candidate said YES! They are starting today! Now the real work of your relationship begins. For an employee-employer relationship to be successful, it takes engagement from both sides. Just like in a dating relationship, the engagement period is critical. Either party can still get "cold feet." As with any engagement, this can be a critical time in the relationship. Engagement involves commitment, involvement, and connection from both the employee and the employer. From their first day with your company, your new employee will need to feel like they are a part of the organization. This starts with your onboarding process.

One day, I was at an appointment, waiting in the company's reception area. Next to me was a smiling young woman who was just starting her employment. She was well-dressed, had a notebook with her, and she approached the front desk of the organization informing the receptionist that this was her first day. The receptionist told her to have a seat and someone would be with her shortly. I watched as the girl sat for thirty minutes waiting to start her day.

Finally, someone from human resources came to get her. As the human resource manager approached her, she said to the girl, "I am sorry, but we didn't know what to do with you. We don't have a desk for you yet, so you will just need to stay in my office for the time being." I watched as the girl who had seemed confident and excited about her new role, suddenly appeared less confident and less excited as she walked behind the manager to figure out where she belonged.

What I'd witnessed at that moment was just sad. Not only did it show a lack of planning, but it devalued the girl. Unfortunately, in that one moment, all the time that was spent developing the relationship with this employee might have just been wiped out by this organization's failure to plan.

It is necessary for an organization to be particularly engaged in their onboarding process. Demonstrating to the new employee the company's excitement to have the employee on board can make a huge difference in their performance and retention. The onboarding process is *critical* to engagement. If you want your employees to be engaged, then they must feel like a part of the organization. Every company I know wants their employees to be engaged; however, few companies are willing to do the work to make sure employees feel important and included.

> "I try to be engaged in the new hire process. Not because it needs to be micromanaged, but more to make sure that the process moves smoothly and quickly for them. You want to have the best possible experience for the new employee as you can from the start."
>
> *Steve Ford, Senior Manager of New Market Development, twenty-plus years' hiring experience, Pharmaceuticals, Capital Equipment, and Medical Device*

The Importance of Onboarding

In the article, "Strategies for Talent Attraction and Onboarding: Optimize your onboarding process to ensure employee success," Sohn writes,

> "To attract and retain the best people, you need to treat every candidate like your most valued customer. This means organizations must provide candidates with a great experience in the earliest stages of the employee lifecycle – attraction and onboarding. HR teams understand that the onboarding process can set the tone for an employee's entire engagement at an organization." [15]

By this, Sohn is arguing that employees become internal customers and should be treated with the utmost respect. We need to position new employees for success from their first day with the organization.

> "If people know they are valued, they will offer more. You can't treat external customers one way and internal customers another way and expect consistent progress."
>
> *Matt Aultman, District Sales Manager, six years' hiring experience, Pharmaceutical Sales*

---

[15] Sohn, D. (2017). Winning Strategies For Talent Attraction And Onboarding: Optimize your onboarding process to ensure employee success. *Leadership Excellence Essentials, 34*(6), 8.

> "HR usually holds a similar role to the recruiter. We are the candidate's first point of contact at the company and they usually feel most comfortable with us. We help them navigate through the process to give them a great experience. This is important because it helps the candidate understand the culture of the organization and decide on whether this is a place, they see themselves."
>
> *Seda Onek, Human Resources Manager, ten-plus years' experience, Medical Device*

We all know that starting something new, like a new job, can be very stressful. During this initial time, feeling like you fit into an organization is crucial. Through proper socialization, an outsider can be transformed into an accepted, productive worker. To do this, the individual needs to understand their role within the organization and be accepted by other members of the staff. An example of this is a promotion. When an individual contributor is promoted into management, they assume the role of manager. However, if their subordinates do not respect them as a manager, then they become less effective in their role. To help prevent this issue, it might also be a good idea to do a one-on-one pre-evaluation of the new employee's new role. Consider sitting down with the individual for thirty minutes to find out what they feel they need to learn to be ready for the job.

> "Share a 30-60-90 day plan that the manager and associate work on together and stick to it. Also good for them to understand the different levels within HR and who to go to for various issues. HR has evolved to more of a self-serve model for associates and managers, so teach the tools early on so the associate knows what to do when they have a question."
>
> *Tracy Barry, Sr. HR Partner, fifteen-plus years' hiring experience, Medical Device, Pharmaceuticals, Financial Services, and Publishing*

> "I outline a formal training and onboarding schedule for the first 4-8 weeks depending on the position."
>
> *Mike DeMuth, VP Sales, fifteen years' hiring experience, Healthcare Information Technology*

In the recruitment industry, our job is to attract talent for organizations. However, as an employer, your job is not only to attract talent but also to keep talent. Beyond that, you should aim to enrich that talent within your organization.

In an article written by Casey and Meredith regarding onboarding, scholars argue,

> "An effective onboarding program is one of the most important training experiences for a new employee. To be as effective as possible, an onboarding program must be rooted in a company's culture, communicating what is important to the organization and providing an employee the skills and knowledge necessary to be successful. Thoughtfully considered and properly benchmarked, an onboarding program prepares new employees for success by supplying them with the tools, resources, and information needed to understand the technical aspects of their role, as well as how to effectively use those aspects to support business goals."[16]

A solid onboarding program will help employee retention. According to the Society for Human Resource Management's (SHRM's) "Human Capital Benchmarking Report", from 2016, companies spend, on average, $4,129 on each hire, and it takes about forty-two days to fill a position. SHRM also reports that "in terms of employee retention, the average employee tenure is eight years, the annual turnover rate is 19 percent and the involuntary turnover rate is 8 percent."[17] What are your retention statistics in comparison? It is not

---

[16] Casey, J., & Meredith, A. (2017). Preparing for Tomorrow's Success: What to Consider When Creating an Effective Onboarding Program. *Training, 54*(2), 42–43.

[17] Average Cost-per-Hire for Companies Is $4,129, SHRM Survey Finds, August 3, 2016 https://www.shrm.org/about-shrm/press-room/press-releases/pages/human-capital-benchmarking-report.aspx Accessed September 23, 2018

easy finding the right people for your organization, but losing employees will cost your company time and money.

As we have discussed, affording a potential candidate the opportunity to preview your organization, such as through an internship or even a ride-along day, can be helpful. It allows the potential employee to see your organization in action. It gives them a glimpse of how they would fit into your organization and its culture prior to coming on board.

> **"We have a program for them to see other parts of the organization. One day a month for nine months they get to interface with other employees in other units to understand the entire organization."**
>
> *Brent Dunn, Vice-President, Office of University Advancement, Executive Director of Missouri State University Foundation, thirty-five years' hiring experience, Higher Education*

Traditionally, new employees are given a ninety-day probationary period. After this time, if they are not performing up to par, the company may decide to terminate their employment. But depending upon the type of position involved, ninety days may not be enough time to evaluate an employee's performance. In sales of capital equipment, it can take up to a year to sell to a major account.

Goals need to be written so that they are achievable. Nothing is worse than giving a new employee unrealistic goals. Setting someone up for failure does just that—produces failure. Creating an organizational culture that encourages success will not only strengthen your team but also your bottom line. Success encourages success. Happy employees will stay with your company and work harder to be even more successful! Turnover is typically higher in companies that have unrealistic expectations. As an example, if your top sales representative has been with the company for five years and is producing X dollars, will a new sales representative be able to produce at that same level within ninety days? Possibly, but are they truly unsuccessful if they don't perform to the same standard or do they just need more time and more coaching? Many organizations have developed quantifiable expectations for new employees in the form of goals or objectives. These are in the form of a measurable criteria which can later be reviewed.

Performance Review

Earlier, I mentioned a type of employee review that I have used in the past. A performance review uses the individual's job description as the basis for the evaluation. A job description and performance review, when used together, creates a great tool in which the employee can better understand the expectations of the employer, and the employer can effectively evaluate the employee based on those expectations. The performance review I have used is a weighted system, meaning it gives a percentage of weight or importance to each duty. For instance, in the case of our recruiting specialists, their expected duties are written on a job description. However, these duties are also written on their performance review and weighted into three categories—research, professional interactions, and management of jobs. Research is weighted the highest at 50 percent, reflecting 50 percent of their job duties, while professional interactions account for 30 percent and management of jobs 20 percent. Each category is then subdivided into key skills and abilities and each is given a maximum score. Merit raises are given based upon the total score the employee receives. See example job description and performance review on the following pages.

Sample Job Description

Position Title: Recruiting Specialist

Reports To: Recruiting Director

Date: July 1, 2018

The statements below are intended to describe the general nature and level of work being preformed by associates assigned to this job. This job description is not intended to be an exhaustive list of all responsibilities, duties, and skills required of associates so classified.

The Recruiting Specialist assists in the research, recruitment, and prescreening of candidates. In this role, the Recruiting Specialist researches both internal and external candidate databases to source for candidates and may prescreen candidates by phone at the request of the Recruiter.

The Recruiting Specialist also assists the organization by targeting new business through internet research of potential new client companies. This includes researching the internet, keeping abreast of industry changes, making introduction calls to companies, and updating and maintaining changes as needed to the company's potential customer databases.

Position Duties:

- Assists in the research of internal and external candidate databases to source appropriate candidates.

- Assists with prescreening potential candidates for qualifications set forth by the client company.

- Assists with emailing pre-screens to candidates, following up, scheduling interviews, and providing updates to candidates as necessary.

- Assists with developing new business through various resources, including online research.

- Assists in development of marketing materials (i.e., mail-outs, email blasts, brochures, etc.)

- Makes contact with potential client companies by identifying an appropriate point of contact.

- Documents phone conversations by adding appropriate notes.

- Documents information on potential client companies that require follow-up.

- Provides on-going lists and appropriate updates on a regular basis to the customer manager database.

- Other duties as assigned.

Sample Performance Review

Performance Review

Employee: _____   Date of Hire: _____

Title: _____

Job Function %	Skills Required	Maximum Points Allowed	Points Achieved
Research (50%)	• Timeliness • Accuracy • Interest Level • Knowledge of Services	15 15 10 10	
Professional Interactions (30%)	• Interactions w/Customers • Interactions w/Supervisor • Interactions w/Peers	10 10 10	
Management of Jobs (20%)	• Completes work assigned • Creativity • Self-starter • Autonomous	10 5 5	
		Total Points	

Comments/Actions:

Points Scale:	Merit Increase	
95-100 points	5%	Merit Increase Achieved: ___%
91-94 points	4 %	Current hourly rate: $
81-90 points	3 %	New hourly rate: $
71-80 points	2 %	Effective Date:
61-70 points	1%	
60 or below	No increase	

Employee Signature: _____   Date: _____

Approved by: _____   Date: _____

This type of system can be implemented at the three-month, six-month, or annual review since it is based on the person's job description. It is a highly effective way of documenting performance. If performance is lacking, it will help you discover any need for further training or other action.

There are many types of performance reviews available. The most important function of a performance review or employee appraisal is feedback. Reviews should be completed during the initial probationary period and then annually. Feedback allows a manager to have open and ongoing communication with their employees. You can essentially become a coach to your employees and watch them grow.

In the long run, a performance review may help you justify any corrective actions and ease your mind that you have done your part as a manager to support your employees. In fact, sitting down with an employee and going through this flowchart may help them understand where they need improvement.

Managerial Reviews - Are you open to it?

Previously, we have talked about building a relationship with your employees. We have discussed how that relationship is similar to a dating scenario. We discovered that both types of relationships, whether personal or business, are based upon the same three ingredients: interest, respect, and ongoing communication. Just like in a personal relationship, if any of these pieces are missing, the relationship can get messy and complicated. As a manager, you should have interest, respect, and ongoing communication with each of your employees. That's a given. Unfortunately, this doesn't always happen. That's why it's important to schedule one-on-one time with each person you supervise. If you are managing a large group of people, this may not be possible, but it works well with small to mid-size teams. During this time, start by discussing how they feel about the work they are doing and how they feel about you as a manager. You may learn a few things about yourself, and your management style that will help you grow.

When we step back and look at all the factors involved in employee engagement, the employee shouldn't be the only one evaluated. It is important to look at the overall engagement of your team and yourself as a manager.

As you continue to develop relationships with your team, remember it is not just about the period of engagement. Engagement is a continual process based upon mutual interest, respect, and ongoing communication between all parties. Engaged employees are generally happy and productive, making your life as a manager easier in the long run.

Succession Planning

One way to keep the fire burning in your employees is to create a career path for them. Like the stages of a rocket, further ignition can help propel a rocket into deep space. Maybe you can further ignite your employees and create a legacy!

You may say that they are already passionate about the company and their job. That's great! They already have the fire burning. The question is, are they working up to their full potential? How long will they be content in the same role? You can help them by setting them up for future successes.

Career planning can help. While it is the responsibility of the employee to ultimately do this themselves, as their leader you can make a big impact by caring about their goals, thereby helping facilitate their advancement within the organization.

When we pre-screen candidates, we ask them why they are interested in making a career move. By far, the top response to this question is that they want to move up in their organization or career, and they do not see that potential with their current employer. This is understandable for smaller organizations. However, from the employee's point of view, the challenge is gone within their current role. This is why succession planning is so effective.

According to John Wright in his article "Does Your Company Have a Leadership Development Plan? 4 things that should not be ignored:"

> "Succession planning means that organizations have a well-thought-out strategy in place to develop leaders' competency and character to suit the needs of the organization, from individual contributors all the way up to the executive team. Moreover, by identifying high-potential future leaders, organizations take steps to ensure their success long into the future by keeping the succession pipeline full and ensuring that leaders are set up for success when the time comes to step into positions of leadership."[18]

Want to create "fire" in your employees? Give them a reason to stay with your company. For example, I had the privilege to work for a community hospice early in my career. I started out in patient care and then moved into a management role. At the time I was promoted, I had an associate's degree in nursing and no management training. My employer was quick to send me to several leadership training programs, and the company encouraged me to finish my bachelor's degree by paying my tuition. This allowed me to not only gain the skills that were needed to manage people, but it also gave me confidence. I stayed with this organization and eventually moved into

---

[18] Wright J. Does Your Company Have A Leadership Development Plan? 4 things that should not be ignored. *Leadership Excellence*. 2018: 35(6):p.18-19.

higher leadership positions. Through my employer's confidence in me, I was able to grow as an individual and my career path continued to keep me engaged.

> "[A leadership development program is] ... invaluable in grooming new talent and retention of great employees."
>
> *Tom Fowler III, Senior Vice President, State Bank of Southwest Missouri, twenty-three year's hiring experience, Banking*

On the same note, also acknowledge the accomplishments of your staff. Identify people within your company that can be placed in leadership positions as your company grows and compliment them.

Consider implementing a leadership training program or other programs that will benefit both your company and your employees for years to come. Ask yourself, are you building leaders who can take your company into the next decade?

> "Investing in leadership development will pay dividends on all fronts – It can look different from one size organization to another. One of the best investments for any organization."
>
> *Rita Wright Gurian, Retired Healthcare Executive – Current Non-Profit & Professional Development Coach, thirty-plus years' hiring experience in Healthcare and Non-Profit*

Preventing Burnout

As we've discussed, you have the potential to create a fire—passion—in others, but to do this, first, you have to create a spark. Think of the Fourth of July.

People gather to watch the sky light up with beautiful fireworks. It's fun watching a child gaze into the dark sky to see it light up with a spectrum of colors. And how much fun are sparklers, right?

From sparklers to rockets, fireworks have one thing in common—they start with a spark. They are ignited! This spark allows each firework to leave the ground and explode, and thereby create joy for all those watching. Sometimes fireworks are beautiful, but if not done correctly they can just fizzle out.

Consider yourself a pyro-technician of people. A pyro-technician is the person responsible for the safe storage, handling, and functioning of fireworks and some explosives. As managers, you are in charge of the safe storage, handling, and functioning of the people you supervise. The fireworks you see will be displayed in your employee's attitudes. When an employee is fizzling out, we call this *burnout* and it can happen to any employee, even yourself. You need to be able to recognize it.

Burnout is defined as "a state of emotional, physical, and mental exhaustion caused by excessive and prolonged stress."[19] It can

---

[19] **Burnout Prevention and Treatment,** Techniques for Dealing with Overwhelming Stress, https://www.helpguide.org/articles/stress/burnout-prevention-and-recovery.htm, Accessed August 12, 2019

happen when we are stressed and feel overwhelmed. It can cause physical ailments—depression, anxiety, and many other issues.

Have you ever interviewed with someone whom you felt had burnout? When you spoke with them, you could tell they weren't passionate or maybe didn't like their own job. How did it make you feel? I bet you left the interview in a hurry and never looked back.

We all want to create a strong, cohesive team, but to do this, we need to realize that it starts with us. If managers are negative about the company, its policies, and products, those attitudes will trickle down to the subordinate employees.

Change can also be a major cause of stress for employees within your organization. In the next chapter, we will discuss its impact upon your people, processes, and outcomes.

CHAPTER ELEVEN

But…It Will Happen

Looking back, you may be able to identify the exact moment when your organization changed. For me, it was when the company I worked for switched from being a non-profit organization to a for-profit organization. For others, it was the departure of a CEO, or a change in technology, or a dip in the economy. No matter what causes a change to occur, the impact of change can be devastating if not handled correctly.

Unplanned change can cause disruption and lead to undue stress for the organization's members. In a personal relationship, people break up or divorce. In an organization, employees can be terminated, laid-off, restructured, downsized, or decide to leave on their own.

One of my favorite things to say during times of change is, "It will all work out." I guess you can say that I am an optimist. One day, I said this to my daughter, and she responded by telling me, "Mom, it may not all work out, but it *will* happen."

No matter how you feel about change, it does *happen* to all of us.

Organizational Earthquakes

Following an earthquake, the United States Department of Interior's Geological Survey Division will determine fault lines. According to its website, faults are not the same as fault lines. Faults are where tension builds between two parts of the Earth's surface causing rocks to move. Fault lines are geographic regions that are known to be prone to faults.[20]

In an organization, faults and fault lines are present. However, it is the fault lines that run deep in an organization's core that must be monitored but often go unnoticed. When considering the fault lines within your organization, keep in mind there are three parts of an organization—people, processes, and outcomes. The effect of change on these parts is important to understand.

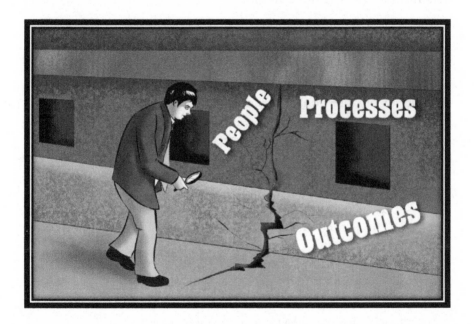

---

[20] United State Department of Interior, Geological Survey Division. Accessed July 9, 2019 through https://www.usgs.gov/faqs/where-are-fault-lines-eastern-united-states-east-rocky-mountains

People, Processes, and Outcomes

Let's consider for a moment that a change is about to occur within your organization. Now, let's look at the impact it could possibly have on your organization, its people, processes and outcomes.

As we move forward with change, ask yourself this question: Which part of the organization (people, processes, or outcomes) will be affected by this change? This is important to understand because when change affects people, different actions may need to be implemented, versus when change affects the processes. Let's discuss more about each of these areas.

People

Often, change impacts people similar to a loss. It may be the loss of normalcy, loss of a leader or loss of business that brings change within an organization. When an unwelcome change occurs, people generally experience reactions similar to the stages of grief. These stages were first identified by Dr. Elisabeth Kubler-Ross. Dr. Kubler-Ross believed these stages were:

Denial: "This can't be happening?"

Anger: "This is not fair!"

Bargaining: "Maybe we can change their mind if we..."

Depression: "Things will never be the same."

Acceptance: "It's going to be okay. I will make it work." [21]

The stages described by Kubler-Ross were not set in any particular order. In fact, she felt most people went in and out of many of these stages. However, she was one of the first to recognize that these

---

[21] Gregory, Christina, PhD, **The Five Stages of Grief,** An Examination of the Kubler-Ross Model https://www.psycom.net/depression.central.grief.html Accessed August 12, 2019

stages were common in people who experienced a loss of some kind or another. As a past hospice nurse, I have seen people go in and out of these various stages during the bereavement process. It can take time, sometimes years, to work through these different feelings when you lose someone you love.

Many of the reactions described by Kubler-Ross can also occur as we experience times of organizational change. Although these are all common reactions to loss, an employee may become angry or depressed when there is a change in their work or career. It is important to keep in mind that change can have a big impact on the morale within the organization if not handled correctly.

How does your organization communicate during times of change? With the heightened use of technology, communication within an organization is often very rapid and impersonal. Leaving a voicemail or sending an email can be detrimental, as these methods do not offer the same benefits as face-to-face communication. Have you ever read an email that left you confused regarding what the person was feeling? In many situations, words can have two distinctly different meanings when written. By hearing inflection and viewing body language, we can better understand each other's feelings. Communication is vital to implementing change within an organization when it comes to rallying employees to accept a pending change.

How do we know when we are communicating effectively? Feedback is key. In many organizations, however, feedback is not always welcomed by upper management. Despite this, feedback within an organization will allow change to occur much smoother than when feedback is avoided. People want to be heard. It is important for us as human beings to feel we were a part of a decision and that our opinion mattered. Leaders can make the mistake of thinking that their subordinates don't care or would not understand the situation. However, an open forum allows for creativity amongst staff.

Take, for instance, a company whose net profit has recently decreased rapidly. The leader's first instinct may be to lay off workers. However, if he or she keeps the staff informed about the bottom line on an ongoing basis, they will be much more likely to make cost-cutting suggestions that may prevent the need to downsize. As managers, it is important for us to train our staff to think like business partners and managers. By getting employees to think like an entrepreneur, you allow them to think outside of the box and show them they are a part of the organization and not just a number. Employees should feel comfortable making suggestions to upper management. When we reach this phase of organizational development, we get the true value of our investment in human capital.

Processes

As mentioned, organizations are built with people, processes, and outcomes. As you determine potential fault lines within your organization, it is important to evaluate and closely monitor your organizational processes. A simple question to ask is, "Does this make sense?" Just because something has always been done a particular way does not mean that it is the simplest, most effective, or cost-saving way to do it now. Another way to view your processes is to monitor issues that arise frequently. Take a few minutes to think about problems that continue to occur in your organization. What are these issues?

I worked for a home healthcare organization as a coordinator of patient care. From the time I started the position, there was a continual fight between the patient care department and the billing department. The manager of the billing department would complain that her department was not being informed of changes in patient status, such as hospitalization and insurance status. This lack of information created billing issues for her department. Over and over, she would complain about the situation. Several months went by and after several run-ins with this manager, I decided to look into the situation. What I found was that although this information was vital to the organization's billing operations, information was lost because it required someone to fill out an unnecessary form. In the massive amount of paperwork that nurses were asked to produce, this form often got forgotten. After some study and review, the answer to the problem became clearer. Streamline the paperwork!

It is vitally important to listen to employee complaints. Although painful at times, when complaints continue to call out the same situation, it is necessary to investigate potential solutions. In the above example, we were able to give the billing department what they needed to bill Medicare, Medicaid, and insurance companies correctly. As an added benefit, we were also able to decrease our own workload.

Outcomes

The last fault line to evaluate is your organization's outcomes. What are the goals of your organization? Are you producing a quality product or offering exceptional service? If not, what are the factors keeping you from doing so?

Quality improvement programs were predominant in the late 1980s through the 1990s. As a statistician and thought-leader, Dr. W. Edward Deming's research on quality was used by many companies to produce better products in a more cost-effective manner. Dr. Deming was a leader in the concepts of continuous quality improvement. His work revolved around producing quality results and lowering costs.

In the new millennium, thought leaders are trying to look at the whole picture. In viewing an organization as a growing, changing entity, they see the need to study organizational development and change within an institution. To produce top products or offer quality services, we must understand the inner workings of our organization first. Just like nurturing an infant into becoming a toddler, then a teenager, and then an adult, organizations need to provide constant care and guidance. Without it, the organization can become an unruly child without a chance for a success in the real world.

Creating a Disaster Recovery Plan

Have you thought about creating a disaster recovery plan for your organization? I know, you think you already have one, right? Most organizations have policy and procedure manuals created to assist employees during times of physical threats such as fire, tornado, earthquakes, hazardous material spills, and so on. But does your organization have a recovery plan set-up to handle the impact of change?

Change within an organization can also be stress-inducing for employees. There are two types of change faced by individuals and organizations. These are planned change and unplanned change. Planned change occurs when the individual is aware that the event or situation will occur within a reasonable amount of time. Planned change allows the individual time to process the event and make necessary arrangements in order to survive the event. Unplanned change occurs when a change happens without warning. An unplanned change does not allow the individual to make any preparation before the event occurs.

During the last economic recession, many were faced with the sudden loss of their job. For most of these individuals, this was an unplanned change. For the few individuals that knew they were going to be downsized, the change was most likely easier to handle. Though unfortunate, fear and legal implications may be keeping us from being open and honest with our employees about change.

As a human being, I think you would agree that it feels much better when we can plan ahead for detours in the road of life. Yet we often expect employees to handle unplanned change without complaining or worrying. No one likes not knowing where they are going or what obstacles lie ahead. Open communication may lessen the issues caused by a change to your organization and allow for better outcomes.

Conclusion

And They Lived… "Happily Ever After"

Thank you for going on this crazy journey with us! Randy and I have been discussing the concepts behind *HIRE with FIRE* for over ten years now. Every day, we work with candidates who are looking forward to the next chapter in their own lives. They are seeking what we all really want in life: to live happily ever after. The phrase *Happily Ever After* is generally used in fables, novels, or children's movies, but the image of what it stands for resonates with all of us. It is a challenge we all face in life. It is most likely the goal we have for our children, our loved ones, and ourselves. Though we cannot control our destiny, we can control how we respond to those challenges and how we treat those around us during those times of change.

Through the past chapters, we have presented you with an overview of the hiring and interview process.

- We discussed developing a strategic hiring plan, how to identify the qualifications (pillars) necessary in a role, and the importance of a written job description.

- Through the acronym FIRE, we focused on four core traits (functionality, integrity, results, and enthusiasm) that can produce success in a new employee. We discussed how to screen, interview, and select candidates based on the FIRE method.

- Through a correlation with personal dating relationships, we discovered that relationships develop during the interview and hiring process and can have an impact on the candidate's perception of the employer. We have also noted that relationships are built upon interest, respect, and ongoing communication between both parties.

- We have also reviewed the importance of onboarding and how to keep employees engaged and motivated.

- We have discussed change and how it can impact your organization's people, processes and outcomes.

Along the way, we hope you have had some fun. It was our intent to broaden your thoughts on interviewing and hiring people because what you do matters! Your role as an interviewer has a direct impact on each person you meet. Some candidates will be at a crossroad in their lives. Some candidates may want to make a career move. Others not so much. Some, through displacement or termination, have been placed in a position in which they are forced to make a change. We have all been there, whether through our own choice or the choice of someone else. We are forced into making a change, and change can be scary.

We hope you will be able to build lasting relationships with the people you interview and hire. Though you cannot hire every candidate you interview, you can still create confidence through your genuine interest, respect, and communication efforts. A recent study by LinkedIn, showed that 83% of candidates say a negative interview experience can change their mind about a role or company they once liked. This is compared to 87% of candidates that say a positive interview experience can change their mind about a role or company they once doubted. [22]

In the long run, it makes all the difference in how your company (and you) are viewed by potential talent.

> "…You can have the greatest product on the market, but if you do not show how important your employees are to that success, you will develop a culture that can destroy a brand and the business. I have seen teams with an average product outperform other organizations in the same market solely based on their positive view of the organization which relates to the way they represent the brand with customers."
>
> *Steve Ford, Senior Manager of New Market Development, twenty-plus years' hiring experience, Pharmaceuticals, Capital Equipment, and Medical Device*

> "Employees talk about their job to their friends and family. You are far more likely to have an employee share a negative comment about their employer than a good one."
>
> *Ericca Zumaya, Human Excellence Generalist, two years hiring experience in Life Sciences/Biotechnology*

---

[22] LinkedIn Talent Solutions (2015) 2015 Talent Trends. Accessed July 10, 2019 through https://business.linkedin.com/content/dam/business/talent-solutions/global/en_us/c/pdfs/global-talent-trends-report.pdf

> **"The employee's state of mind is reflected in the enthusiasm during live customer interfaces and timing of follow-up."**
>
> *Marc Waldman, VP Business Development, twenty years' hiring experience, Medical Device*

Candidates will visit your company's website and review social media platforms to determine how you treat your employees. According to another study, 79% of job seekers are likely to use social media in their job search[23]. With websites that allow candidates and employees to review and rate your company, your reputation has never mattered more! Your company's brand is more than just the products you sell—it is also your company's culture, how you treat your employees, and the people you interact with outside of your organization (the candidates you don't hire). Today, this is termed as your employer brand.

By enhancing a candidate's experience during the interview and hiring process, you will attract top talent to your company and promote your employer brand. Your company's reputation as a great place to work will make recruiting fast and easy. We believe that through the *HIRE with FIRE* strategies, your company will hire engaged employees who will drive more business and exceed your customers' expectations.

> **"Employees are the best marketing vehicles for all organizations. Their testimony will have huge creditability and their work experience will shape their belief."**
>
> *Rita Wright Gurian, Retired Healthcare Executive – Current Non-Profit & Professional Development Coach, thirty-plus years' hiring experience in Healthcare and Non-Profit*

---

[23] Barac, Dino. 2016. *Twelve Stats Every HR Professional Needs to Know About Employer Branding.* Accessed July 10, 2019. https://www.linkedin.com/pulse/employer-branding-statistics-inforgraphic-dino-bara.

It is our hope that by using these strategies, the relationships you build with your employees and potential employees will last a lifetime and that you will live *Happily Ever After*!

REFERENCES

Alden, A. (2019, January 27). *The Nevada Silver Rush*. Retrieved 09 20, 2019, from https://www.thoughtco.com/nevada-silver-rush-1440699

Barac, D. (2016). *Twelve Stats Every HR Professional Needs to Know About Employer Branding*. Retrieved July 10, 2019, from https://www.linkedin.com/pulse/employer-branding-statistics-inforgraphic-dino-bara

Burnout Prevention and Treatment. (n.d.). *Techniques for Dealing with Overwhelming Stress*. Retrieved August 12, 2019, from https://www.helpguide.org/articles/stress/burnout-prevention-and-recovery.htm

Casey, J. &. (2017). Preparing for Tomorrow's Success: What to Consider When Creating an Effective Onboarding Program. *Training*, 54 (2), 42-43.

Cohen, J. (2012). *Human Ancestors Tamed Fire Earlier Than Thought*. Retrieved July 8, 2019, from https://www.history.com/news/human-ancestors-tamed-fire-earlier-than-thought

Dimock, M. (2019, January 17). *Defining generations: Where Millennials end and Generation Z begins*. Retrieved August 24, 2019, from https://www.pewresearch.org/fact-tank/2019/01/17/where-millennials-end-and-generation-z-begins/

Gallup. (2017). *State of the American Workplace*. Retrieved July 11, 2019, from https://www.gallup.com/workplace/238085/state-american-workplace-report-2017.aspx

Gregory, C. P. (n.d.). *The Five Stages of Grief, An Examination of the Kubler-Ross Model.* Retrieved August 12, 2019, from https://www.psycom.net/depression.central.grief.html

Grensing-Pophal, L. (2018, February 26). *How to Handle 5 Generations in the Workplace.* Retrieved July 8, 2019, from https://hrdailyadvisor.blr.com/2018/02/26/handle-5-generations-workplace/

Indeed. (2019, August 26). *The Ghosting Guide: An Inside Look at Why Job Seekers Disappear.* Retrieved August 27, 2019, from http://blog.indeed.com/2019/08/26/ghosting-guide/

LinkedIn Talent Solutions. (n.d.). *2015 Talent Trends.* Retrieved July 10, 2019, from https://business.linkedin.com/content/dam/business/talent-solutions/global/en_us/c/pdfs/global-talent-trends-report.pdf

Mathis, R. L. (2008). *Human Resource Management* (Twelfth ed.). Mason, OH: South-Western Cengage Learning.

Merriam-Webster. (n.d.). *Merriam Webster.* Retrieved August 23, 2019, from https://www.merriam-webster.com/dictionary/relationship

Merriam-Webster. (n.d.). *Merriam-Webster.* Retrieved July 8, 2019, from https://www.merriam-webster.com/dictionary/interviewing

Merriam-Webster. (n.d.). *Merriam-Webster.* Retrieved July 8, 2019, from https://www.merriam-webster.com/dictionary/ghosting

Merrill, D. W. (1981, January 15). *Personal Styles and Effective Performance.* CRC Press Merrill Reid

Perkins, C. (n.d.). *https://smallbusiness.chron.com/diamond-model-organizational-effectiveness-73563.html*. Retrieved September 22, 2019, from Diamond Model for Organizational Effectiveness

SHRM (2016, August 3). *Average Cost-per-Hire for Companies Is $4,129*. Retrieved September 23, 2018, from https://www.shrm.org/about-shrm/press-room/press-releases/pages/human-capital-benchmarking-report.aspx

Sohn, D. (2017). Winning Strategies For Talent Attraction And Onboarding: Optimize your onboarding process to ensure employee success. *Leadership Excellence Essentials*, 34 (6), 8.

United States Department of Interior, Geological Survey Division. (n.d.). Retrieved July 9, 2019, from https://www.usgs.gov/faqs/where-are-fault-lines-eastern-united-states-east-rocky-mountains

Wright, J. (2108). Does Your Company Have A Leadership Development Plan? 4 things that should not be ignored. *Leadership Excellence*, 35 (6): p. 18-19.

INDEX

A

B

C

D

E

F

G

H

I

J

K

L

M

N

O

P

Q

R

S

Sexual harassment · 4
Society for Human Resource Management (SHRM) · 116
Soul mate · 19, 22
Spark · 57, 76, 81, 125
Steward, Reggie · vii, 66, 75, 92
Succession planning · 124
Surface interviewing · 88

T

Thank you note · 83, 84
Top performers · 19, 57
Traditionalists · 99

U

U.S. Equal Employment Opportunity Commission · 3
Uniform Guidelines on Employee Selection Procedures · 4
United States Department of Interior's Geological Survey Division · 128

W

Waldman, Marc · vii, 21, 75, 92, 139
Wright Gurian, Rita · vii, 20, 74, 91, 125, 139

Z

Zumaya, Ericca · vii, 74, 93, 108, 138

ABOUT THE AUTHORS

Denise Wilkerson is the founder and CEO of Global Edge Recruiting Associates, LLC. Randy Wilkerson, her husband and business partner, is the Vice-President of Executive Search and Recruitment Services. Founded in 1997, Global Edge Recruiting® is a nationally recognized executive search firm specializing in the recruitment of medical device, pharmaceutical, biotechnology, dental and veterinary sales and marketing representatives.

More About Denise Wilkerson

Born in NYC and raised in a small town in Missouri, Denise started her career in nursing -first in oncology, where she worked in the hospital as a staff nurse, and then for a hospice where she managed a team of nurses. After managing a large women's healthcare clinic for a local hospital, she decided to start her own business and opened Global Edge Recruiting in 1997. Since that time, Denise has assisted hundreds of Fortune 500 and small start-up companies by recruiting their top talent and assisting them with day-to-day human resource and organizational development needs.

Denise is also passionate about helping job seekers through various types of career transitions. As a career counselor, she assists job seekers with resume development, interviewing skills, and career management. Denise enjoys sharing her knowledge with others which is evident by her company's blog and social media. She has contributed to multiple publications and books on recruitment.

On a professional note, Denise has a Bachelor's degree in Nursing, as well as a Master's in Human Resource Development and a Senior Professional Human Resources certification (SPHR). Her love for innovative medical products and devices, as well as her passion for assisting individuals with career development led her to healthcare recruitment. She has over thirty years of hiring experience in general healthcare, sales and marketing.

More about Randy Wilkerson

A native of Springfield, Missouri, Randy is the son of two educators. His mother was a teacher and high school counselor in the Springfield area and his father was a high school principal and state representative. Growing up, his parents emphasized the importance of education, something that has stuck with him throughout life.

While attending Missouri State University, Randy received a teaching certification in business and general science, along with his undergraduate degree in both marketing and management. Later, he completed his Masters of Business Administration at Webster University. He has a private pilot's license and a real estate broker's license. Randy loves to educate others along with being in front of a group. Early in his career, he taught adult education courses in real estate.

Randy Wilkerson joined Global Edge Recruiting in 2007 as Vice President, Executive Search and Recruitment. Prior to joining Global Edge, Randy was a successful sales representative. He worked for several Fortune 500 companies including Xerox Corporation, Roche Pharmaceuticals and Janssen Pharmaceuticals, a division of Johnson and Johnson. Randy's extensive background in sales and marketing assists clients in the recruitment and development of sales teams. Randy has over fifteen years of hiring experience in general healthcare sales and marketing.

Personally, Randy is known for his sense of humor which is evident in many of his writings. He is also very technical, and enjoys a good repair challenge. He rebuilds old jukeboxes and pinball machines for fun. In addition to these hobbies, he likes to spend time at the lake and working on the family's ranch.

On a Personal Note

Randy and Denise reside near Springfield, Missouri in the beautiful Ozark Mountains. They've been married for over 32 years and have one amazing daughter, Lindsey, and a funny, dachshund-terrier mixed dog named Patches. They are currently writing their second book, *INTERVIEW with DESIRE and GET HIRED!* designed to assist candidates.

For More Information, visit

www.dandyworx.com
www.globaledgerecruiting.com

Made in the USA
Las Vegas, NV
20 May 2021

23413045R00100